STOP *Wandering* THE CORRIDORS OF YOUR MIND

A Personal Testimony of God's Unfailing Love and His Desire to Set His People Free

Dan,

It was great working with you! Thanks for your helpfulness and expertise. May you continue to have success in the future.

As for the book, may you find the same hope & peace I did in whatever storms of life you are facing.

Bill

STOP Wandering THE CORRIDORS OF YOUR MIND

A Personal Testimony of God's Unfailing Love and His Desire to Set His People Free

BILL KER

REDEMPTION PRESS

Published by Redemption Press, PO Box 427, Enumclaw, WA 98022. Toll Free (844) 2REDEEM (273-3336)

Redemption Press is honored to present this title in partnership with the author. The views expressed or implied in this work are those of the author. Redemption Press provides our imprint seal representing design excellence, creative content and high quality production.

ISBN 13: 978-1-63232-626-3 (Soft Cover)
          978-1-63232-629-4 (ePub)
          978-1-63232-630-0 (Mobi)

Library of Congress Catalog Card Number: 2016942761

Contents

Acknowledgments

I WANT TO thank my family and friends for all of your love and support. Your prayers and encouragement cheered me on. Most of all, I want to thank my wife. You showed me the meaning of true loyalty and faithfulness. You never gave up on me. You were there for me in my darkest days. And you took my hand as I took my first steps in freedom.

Foreword

B ILL KER HAS written an engaging, brutally honest, and often funny account of tragically universal human experience—the construction of a mental prison based on shame, embarrassment, twisted self-worth, and the matter-of-fact results of real sin. His book guides you stage by stage through his life and the fabrication of his incarceration. No matter who you are, you will find yourself, and some of your own experience in these pages. I hope you will also find the same freedom that Bill did—the absolute destruction of your artificial prison by Jesus Christ. To know about freedom and to actually possess freedom are very different things. The latter is the only promise that matters. So if the Son liberates you [makes you free men], then you are really and unquestionably free (John 8:36).

Christian Lindbeck—Senior Associate Pastor and School of Ministry & Global Discipleship

CHAPTER ONE

Called Out

LIKE EVERY OTHER Sunday morning, I awoke crushed by the weight of my burdens. I again fantasized about jumping off the 325-foot Selah Creek Bridge in Yakima, Washington. The monsters in the black hole of my mind taunted me.

How much longer could I endure?

Little did I know of the miracle that was about to transpire. God changed the course of my life that summer Sunday.

At the end of a service in 2008, Pastor Aaron asked for people to come forward for prayer. I went. I closed my eyes and bowed my head before him. He remained quiet. After several moments I opened my eyes and looked at him. He gazed at me with intensity.

Was he mad at me? Did I do something wrong? What's going on?

Pastor Aaron laid his hands on my head. "Bill, this is what the Lord says. It's time to stop wandering the corridors of your mind. For too long you have been roaming around inside the prison of your mind. For too long you have been isolated. For too long you have been alone. It's time to be free."

I stepped back. Pastor Aaron had violated me. He invaded my innermost thoughts without my permission. I thought, *How did you know about the corridors of my mind, Pastor Aaron? You don't know about them. Nobody knows about them. You are trespassing.*

For the next few minutes, I felt like the Beast from *Beauty and the Beast* when Belle entered the forbidden West Wing.

Within an hour my anger subsided. I realized the Holy Spirit had revealed the words Pastor Aaron spoke to me. At home, I sat at my kitchen table. After everything happened in quick fashion at church, I had a chance to think.

I closed my eyes. I visualized the voice of Jesus speaking through a hurricane. With authority He declared, *Bill come out of your prison. You don't belong here. Let me have total access and free reign in your entire mind. I want to rescue you. It's time to be free.*

His voice, a sweet melody to my spirit, quieted my torment, sorrow, and shame.

Although God called me out of my spiritual Alcatraz, I couldn't leave. Deeply broken, I resisted freedom. For the next four years I remained a prisoner. I continued to lay brick after brick to build the individual prison cells and endless corridors.

God, though, had a different plan. He gently set me on a path towards deliverance. He never forgot His promise of freedom to me.

About a year after Pastor Aaron laid hands on me, I caught Pastor Jentezen Franklin's appearance on TBN. His message focused on fasting. He detailed his church's annual twenty-one-day fast. Their dedication, devotion, and commitment amazed me.

While Pastor Jentezen spoke, the Holy Spirit convicted me. *It's time for you to fast.*

"There is no way I can do that."

I knew little about fasting or its significance. Especially for twenty-one days. With my small stature I'd shrivel up and disappear before day ten.

I bought Pastor Jentezen's book, *Fasting: Opening the Door to a Deeper, More Intimate, More Powerful Relationship with God.* I didn't fast for twenty-one days. I opted for a three-day, water-only fast.

During my fast, I read Pastor Jentezen's book. I learned about radical testimonies and unbelievable miracles in his church. I sat at the kitchen table on the final morning of my fast. I read the last few pages of the book. When I finished the Holy Spirit said, *I want you to write a book and you will title it* Stop Wandering the Corridors of Your Mind. *It will be a testimony to my power in your life and I will use it as a tool of ministry to help set my children free.*

Me? Write a book? I don't read books. How can I write one? I scowled and bombarded Him with pointed questions. *Do you know who I am and what I have done? Who am I and how am I qualified to write a book? Won't this book just disappear in the ocean of all the other great books already written?*

I tried to convince Jesus of His mistake for choosing me. I didn't receive answers to my demanding questions. For the next two-and-a-half years God pestered me about the book. I gave Him excuses for why I wouldn't write it.

Until one day I surrendered my will to His. During my hour-and-half commute home I shouted in the cab of my truck, "Okay, Lord, I'll do it."

I finally said yes. Now what? Aware of the numerous books written by Spirit-filled Christians, the task of writing seemed daunting. I lacked the necessary strength and ability. I didn't have sufficient knowledge and experience. I needed the Lord's wisdom and direction.

In late January 2013 I sat at a small table in our church cafeteria. I held a pen in my hand. A blank notebook laid on the table. I stared at the empty pages and prayed, "Jesus, what do you want me to write and how do you want me to write it? I don't even know where to start."

Within a few minutes He revealed the entire outline and theme of my book. The words poured into my mind. I wrote furiously. About an hour passed. I jotted down in bullet points the outline, theme, and major events of my life. Jesus revealed how deep into my past he wanted me to go.

He showed me the issues I needed to address. What He wanted me to write scared me. He wanted me to expose intimate details of my life. I whimpered, *Lord, you want me to tell everyone about everything I struggled with?*

Yes, He replied.

But I know some people will think I am disgusting and offensive. I am certain they will say things like "How could he do that?" or "I am sure glad I am not that kind of person" or "I hope my kids never experience that."

With a soft voice Jesus calmed my worries. *Do you trust me?*

His question provided comfort. He assured me of contentment through obedience. Jesus encouraged me to be transparent and genuine about my brokenness. He wanted to convey the power of God's transformational love.

I wanted people to know Jesus is real. I wanted people to know He is relevant. I wanted people to know He cares about our pain and suffering.

But, did I want to get uncomfortable for His greater plan at the expense of my reputation? No.

But I wanted to break free from the prison of my mind.

CHAPTER TWO

The Foundation of Torment Laid

MY PARENTS WERE born and raised in the United States. They graduated college together and married in 1964. They resided in nine different countries before moving to the island of Mindanao, Philippines. With a son and daughter of their own, they decided to adopt. I was born in Baguio, Philippines in late winter 1975. The hospital placed me in the Heart of Mary Villa orphanage outside of Manila. Nine weeks later my parents adopted me. I am thankful my biological parents didn't choose to abort me.

At six months old my hip sockets were displaced. My feet lay flat on their sides when I lay on my back. My mom twisted my legs inward every day for several months. I also wore special shoes connected to a bar. The apparatus kept my legs straight when I slept. But I took my first steps at thirteen months old.

My family left the Philippines in early spring 1976. For six months we traveled to Hong Kong, Israel, Greece, Italy, Spain, and England. Towards the end of 1976 we moved back to the United States. My sister and brother were in third grade and kindergarten. I was almost two years old.

My dad landed a job in Walla Walla, Washington with Western Farm Service. We stayed in Walla Walla until the spring of 1977. He then joined the company Lamb Weston. We moved to Kennewick, Washington.

We lived in an amazing house. It seemed like Disneyland for the almost thirteen years I lived there. Built in the late sixties or early seventies and approximately 3,600 square feet, the house contained four levels: a full basement, a ground level, a mid-level and an upstairs. Different carpet covered the floor in each room. I remember that some colors were hideous. A bright red ground floor with dark green paisley patterns. A dark pea-green soup color in the basement. The basement resembled more of a pad than carpet.

Did I care about interior decor at such a young age? Nope. The underground basement with no windows served as the family and neighborhood playground. We played Chutes and Ladders, Candy Land, Life, Operation and many other fun games. My brother practiced WWF moves on me and my friends. Painful moves like body slams, suplexes, and pile drivers. My friends and I feared the camel clutch the most. We loved building forts and castles and all kinds of fun things.

I spent most of my outdoor time in the back yard. Three sections divided the yard. A huge covered patio in the middle, a separate yard on the right and separate yard on the left. All kinds of trees, bushes, flowers and plants grew in the yard. Maple trees, apricot trees, snowball trees, Concord grape vines, arborvitae bushes and mint plants to name a few.

A variety of wildlife also inhabited our backyard. Birds, squirrels, frogs, moles, and an occasional possum or two. The yard on the right had a small pond with a rock waterfall. Frogs and fish my brother caught from the Columbia River lived there. Discovery Channel could have done a *Planet Earth* series on our backyard.

During my early childhood I struggled with health issues. At two and a half, I contracted pneumonia. I stayed in the hospital for several days. I have a memory of lying in an incubator in the hospital. The doctor leaned over, smiled and gave me a grape popsicle.

Because of the pneumonia I developed idiopathic thrombocytopenic purpura (ITP), a blood-clotting disorder that led to excessive bruising and bleeding. Normal daily activities and playing left deep bruises on my skin.

In my twenties, my mom shared a story about my ITP. One day she received a knock on the front door from a police officer.

"Ma'am, can I please see your son."

"Why? Is something wrong? Did something happen?"

"We have reports about concerns of child abuse."

Someone saw me covered in bruises with my mom at the grocery store. They assumed she beat me. Disgusted by the thought of abuse, she explained my condition to the police officer. The seriousness of the illness required me to wear protective head gear. A head injury could have led to a brain hemorrhage and death.

At the age of three I wore a burgundy-colored motorcycle helmet everywhere I went. Big for my little head, it looked like a shiny sweet cherry. Three silver buttons wrapped around the front for a snap on plastic visor. I sweated a lot in the summer when I played.

I consider my pre-school through fifth grade years as somewhat of a typical American childhood. I didn't grow up in the information and technology age. I played four to six hours outside at times with ease.

Endless amounts of energy flowed from my body. Most people labeled me hyperactive. I loved to show off. My parents constantly told me to settle down.

I played with dirt clods, torched various kinds of bugs with a magnifying glass and rode my bicycle. I also loved to play hooky bob in the winter, a game I used to play when the streets were covered in snow. To play, I hid behind a bush or parked car near an intersection. When a vehicle pulled up and stopped, I snuck up behind it. I grabbed onto the bumper or tailgate. I positioned my feet like skis. The vehicle accelerated and pulled me down the street.

My friends and I enjoyed the game. We disregarded personal safety for the thrill. Over time we upgraded to metal saucers and different kinds of sleds. I reintroduced the game in my junior and senior years of high school. I used our family's inner tube meant for our boat. Curbs, parked cars, and other immovable objects, put a "dent" in our activities.

My active family also kept me busy. My parents loved to travel all over the West Coast in our 1970s Shasta camper. We frequented places like Lake McCall, Jubilee Lake, Mount Rainier, and Thousand Trails. We white-water rafted on the Snake River, Clearwater River, and Salmon River.

A family friend owned a time-share cabin in the Blue Mountains in Oregon. I loved the cabin. It was my favorite place nestled in the woods away from civilization. A freshwater creek ran next to the cabin. I fished for trout, hunted crawdads and built rock dams. I flung rocks at water skipper bugs. I explored the forest trails on my bike. The woods hosted my playground of adventures.

I also enjoyed my indoor time. I relished TV. *Silver Spoons*, *Dukes of Hazzard*, *The Cosby Show*, *The A-Team*, *Knight Rider*, *ALF*, *Different Strokes*, *Facts of Life*, *Who's the Boss*, *Growing Pains*, and *Family Ties* were some of my favorites. Cartoons like *Looney Tunes*, *Tom and Jerry*, *Transformers*, *He-Man*, *BraveStarr*, *Justice League*, and *The Smurfs* captivated my attention.

My dad bought the family an Atari and an Apple IIc computer. Both of them demanded hours of attention. My brother and I engrossed ourselves in Oregon Trail, Asteroids, and Raiders of the Lost Ark.

Many of my friends envied me. My parents provided me with a beautiful life. I lived in a stable home, in a safe environment, and with a wonderful family. But I recognized something wrong inside me. On the outside people saw an energetic and exuberant boy. On the inside I started a pattern of isolation.

At the age of four or five I became familiar with sorrow. I built walls and recited lines about my worthlessness. I didn't understand why. I didn't understand where feelings of hopelessness and despondency came from. I didn't know how they happened or what created them. I simply knew a war raged inside my mind.

But, in the midst of my sorrow, God revealed His love for me. He revealed Himself to me in subtle ways. I recognized His voice in the sound of white water as it rushed over the rocks. I felt Him touch my face in the gentle spring breeze. I saw His splendor in the beauty of the forest.

Jesus never left me alone. He accompanied me out of the basement when I finished playing. The light switch was at the bottom of the basement stairs. I feared the pitch black when the lights were off. The moment I turned the lights off I leapt up the stairs like a gazelle. At the top of the stairs I turned around and faced the basement.

With outstretched arms I said, "I love you Jesus Christ, God, good angels and guardian angels." How did I know to say that? Who taught me to say that? I don't know. I don't remember if anyone did.

By age six my thoughts were mixed and confused. In one moment, loneliness and despair battered me. In another moment, the love of Jesus rescued me. How did my mind become a battlefield? Was there something I did wrong to deserve this?

CHAPTER THREE

Tortured Soul

MY ELEMENTARY YEARS were riddled with trauma. Fear and the insatiable desire for social acceptance consumed me. I attended two different elementary schools in Kennewick, Washington—Canyon View Elementary and Southgate Elementary. I interacted well with most of the kids. I played the popular games at recess: four square, red rover, and duck duck goose.

But my small size of maybe sixty pounds made me an easy target for ridicule, teasing, and jokes. The bigger kids didn't pick me to play games like football at recess. I often heard, "I don't want Bill on my team. He's too small."

Rejection stalked me beyond the playground. Many opportunities were missed to play capture the flag or kick the can with my older family friends. They denied me with emphatic responses, "No, you are too puny. You'll just slow us down."

My timid demeanor and small stature also attracted bullies. I developed a spidey sense for bullies. Sometimes a bully would tease me at the urinal. I cringed when I heard, "What's the matter, your thing too small?" So I learned to hold my pee because I didn't want a bully to follow me into the bathroom.

The size of the boy determined the intensity of harassment. I dreaded being cornered and pushed against walls. But I feared being tackled and pinned down the most. With my arms and legs immobilized, a bully would sit on my chest. He leaned over my face and let a string of saliva ooze out of his mouth. He'd let it hang down to about one inch from my mouth. The bully tried to suck up the saliva just before it touched me. Most of the time he failed and saliva landed on my face or mouth.

Even some girls weren't afraid of me. Class dismissed early on a Wednesday for Thanksgiving break in fifth grade. Several inches of snow blanketed the ground. I exploded out of the classroom door with jubilation. I manhandled the closest kid to me and shouted, "It snowed. It snowed."

"Stop pushing me and knock it off," he yelled. His girlfriend took exception to me laying hands on her boyfriend. She sprinted towards me and pushed me. "He told you to knock it off."

"Get away from me." I pushed her back and she fell in the snow.

She jumped up and charged at me. She nailed me on the nose with a right hook. Her punch stunned me. A split second later a left hook hit me on the nose again. She punched like Mike Tyson. Blood dripped out of my nose.

A crowd of spectators gathered around. I gritted my teeth and lunged at her. I tackled her to the ground. I landed a barrage of left and right hooks into her ribs and side of her head. I got my revenge like Ralphie did in *The Christmas Story*.

Even though I won the fight, I lost reputation. Word spread like wildfire. "Bill got beat up by a girl." The embarrassment haunted me the rest of fifth grade.

The constant bombardment of cruel words and bullying devastated me. I believed my mom birthed a mistake. Day after day I recited in my mind, *You are garbage. You are worthless. Just die already.* A garden of toxic thoughts cultivated in my mind. Things planted in the garden sprouted mental prison cells. Charlie Brown and I would have been good buddies.

How did I fight back? I didn't. I found places to be alone and cry. I released my anger and frustration out on younger and smaller kids in my neighbor. People bullied and hurt me so I bullied and hurt others.

I have since learned to be aware of the words I speak. Speaking life is like a spiritual mouth wash. Speaking death is like halitosis.

I liken ill words to morning breath. The kind that smells like a small rodent crawled into your mouth at night and died. You lean over to your spouse to say good morning. You present a kiss. She turns pale and has the urge to blow chunks. You get a stern order to sprint to the bathroom. "Rinse with mouthwash or sleep in the garage next time."

Despite my grade school anguish I managed to get my first girlfriend. We knew each other for a couple years. We made our relationship official in fifth grade. She called me one day on the phone around Christmas time. She said her mom had bought mistletoe and she wanted to see me. She hinted several times for me to come to her house. Naïve and innocent, I didn't understand the proposition. Frustrated, she said, "Come over to my house and stand under the mistletoe. I want to kiss you."

Afraid and speechless I replied, "Umm, let me ask my mom first."

She gasped. "He's asking his mom? He's asking his mom."

I handed the phone to my mom. "She wants to know if you can take me to her house so I can stand under the mistletoe and kiss her." My mom got on the phone and scolded her for inappropriate behavior.

Rumors spread about me again at school. "Bill is a prude." My girlfriend dumped me after that incident.

But the girlfriend experience left an imprint. I liked the allure of physical attraction. I explored my curiosity. But my curiosity quickly became unhealthy.

I first looked at pornographic magazines at nine or ten. Not long after, I discovered pornographic films. I developed a perverted view of a relationship between a boy and girl.

As time passed I shared my thoughts and desires with neighborhood girls. We touched each other and exposed our bodies. Some were younger than me and others were older. I also shared my curiosity with some friends that were boys. We did the same things I did with the girls. I didn't understand what I did. But I tried to express my feelings from what I learned.

Around age eleven or twelve I experienced unwanted sexual advances. One of the dads in the neighborhood molested me. He also tricked me into exposing myself to him. An older boy from a family I knew also seduced me. But because of my previous behavior, molestation didn't seem unusual. Sexual perversion seemed normal.

I needed something to give me value and affirmation. I thought I would find self-worth and love in sexual exploration. My sexual encounters and elementary trauma mashed together. A dark cloud overshadowed my life.

Even family pets were not immune to my dark cloud. I loved Skipper, our fifteen-pound black poodle. One summer day I slid down a slip and slide in our front yard. Skipper sniffed around and explored the yard. He poked his head into the bushes. He flushed a small flock of quail out.

He then chased them into the street next to our yard. I couldn't stop him. A split second later a car smashed him. I witnessed the entire event. I sprinted into the middle of the street and fell at his body. I screamed at the car at the top of my lungs.

I blamed myself for my dog's death. I didn't protect him, I failed him. I punished myself. *It's your fault Skipper is dead.* The sound of the impact, his high-pitched yelp, and the twitching of his body replayed in my head. Not a good memory.

But, in the midst of my anguish, Jesus never abandoned me. I didn't understand His love then. But I sensed His presence. He wrapped His arms around me. A pattern of encounters with Jesus began.

After the loss of Skipper subsided, we adopted a new dog. I loved Cha Cha, too, a poodle/pekingese mix. By far my favorite childhood pet. Cha Cha became my counselor. I often poured out my pain and sorrow to her. Some days I hid alone with her. I cried my eyes out until they swelled shut. She comforted me and licked my salty tears. We had an unbreakable bond for the almost eighteen years she lived.

I found other ways to cope with my internal struggle. I explored the mysteries of fire. Fire sedated the storms in my mind. I turned my backyard sandbox into a fire laboratory. Dry grass, dead leaves or sticks served as fuel. I soon upgraded to gasoline for more excitement.

I snuck into my garage. The five gallon gasoline can intended for our lawnmower and motorcycle beckoned me. I spelled my name in the sand with a stick and dug little canals for the gas. I lit the gas on fire and marveled at the display.

My brother and I invented a new gasoline game. Pour gas on an open flame. Let the fire travel up the spout but not go inside the can. I failed. The flame ignited the gas that spilled on and around the can. Terrified, I dropped the can on the ground and ran to get my dad. My brother kicked the can over. Somehow the flames extinguished. My brother saved me from fire catastrophe a few other times.

But the danger of fire didn't deter me. The allure of fire distracted my thoughts. One summer day my neighbor came to my house. She said, "I got some matches. Want to go to the field and light them?"

I liked her and wanted to impress her. I didn't hesitate to say yes. We rode our bikes to a field behind my house. Dry dead cheat grass covered the field. Common sense and consequences didn't exist in my brain. Cocky and confident, I lit the first match. A breeze picked up and the fire spread out of control.

She screamed. I tried to remain calm. "I'll put it out." I threw chunks of discarded sod on the fire. A few moments later I gave up. We jumped on our bikes and raced home. I burst through my front door. I dove on the floor in front of my mom. Shocked and in a panicked voice she said, "What's the matter, are you hurt?" When I squeaked out I lit the field on fire she called the fire department.

My mom put me in her car and we drove up to the field. The fire trucks and fireman sprayed water on the fire. Neighbors who evacuated their homes watched from the street. I ignored common sense and safety to impress a neighborhood girl. We didn't hang out after the field burned. Scowls from the neighbors reminded me of my stupidity.

Although fire didn't scare me, many other things did. In first grade my mom drove me to school. In second grade I rode my bike. I convinced my mom I had amassed enough confidence to go alone. But I trembled in fear. I pedaled at a snail's pace. I hoped my mom would change her mind and pick me up. I coasted down the small hill towards the main intersection between the road and school parking lot.

The duty-guard waved me over and I cowered. My insecurities, failures and mistakes shouted at me *You're not good enough, You're so small, Nobody likes you.* Nauseated, I turned my bike around. I raced home crying. Fear enveloped me each time I approached the same intersection.

Eventually I tolerated the fear. But I continued to search for ways to fit in. I listened to kids of all ages tell scary stories. Stories riddled with evil, death and torment. The supernatural fascinated me. I participated more and more in it. I frequently stayed overnight at friend's houses. We watched horror movies and told ghost stories. Some nights we snuck out and walked through the local cemetery.

My reputation elevated. I became the ghost whisperer for many of my friends. I immersed and saturated my thoughts in tales of macabre. I sensed the evil behind my behavior. But I didn't understand it. The dark terrified me. I avoided being alone in the woods. Nightmares were a common occurrence.

I basked in the attention I received. I craved more ways to get it. I scared people, made them laugh, and showed off. I perceived value and acceptance came from attention.

I showed off for the popular girls I liked while on a field trip. Our class went to Whitman Mission near Walla Walla, Washington. I annoyed them with my immature antics and hyperactive gestures. My teacher with a creepy red mustache grabbed me by the back of my hair and shirt. He gritted his teeth. "I have had enough of you." He hauled me off to the bus. I waited alone until the field trip ended.

My strategy backfired. Gossip of, "Did you hear what Bill did? He got so busted" spread across the school again. I still carry the war wounds on my butt from my parent's discipline.

I searched for attention everywhere I turned. Kids treasured Valentine's Day in elementary school. Girls and boys wrote notes on cards that fit into tiny white envelopes. The cards and words on the Necco candy hearts carried tremendous significance.

Nobody wanted to be the kid with the least amount of cards. I compared card totals with other kids in the class. I wanted to have the most. But someone always received more. Devastated, I attributed my lack of cards to a lack of love. I tried to earn love based on a quantity of Valentine's Day cards.

I tried to earn love in my own family. I believed I needed to fight and compete for their attention. With an older brother and sister I put forth more effort during family gatherings. Especially when all thirteen first cousins on my dad's side were together. We often celebrated Thanksgiving and Christmas at my grandparent's home in Quincy, Washington. I established my rank and position to prove myself to the younger and older cousins.

For almost thirty years we've celebrated a one-week family reunion at the Oregon Coast. I still feel the urge to prove to everyone I have it all together. To show them my family is provided for and I'm not a total failure.

My desire for attention knew no bounds. I engaged in risky behavior to get it. I egged houses, TP-ed yards and vandalized cars. Then I discovered how to steal. I learned the techniques of the trade. I became proficient at stealing small items.

I honed my skills in the clubhouse locker room at a golf course near our home. I partnered with someone who showed me how to sneak in undetected. Inside the locker room were stacks of boxes full of paper pull-tabs. The pull tabs were sold at bowling alleys and bars. We left with several boxes each.

I also stole chromies off the valve stems of bicycles and car tires. The good ones were composed of actual chrome. My posse of friends scavenged different neighborhoods and grocery store parking lots. After a couple hours we escaped with our booty of treasure bags full of chromies. We bartered with them to trade toys and goods with other neighborhood kids. Doing the wrong thing overruled the right thing. You were cool if you stole.

But chasing after Al Capone's lifestyle didn't fill the empty void in my heart. The cycle of chaos in my mind manifested into nail biting. I chewed on them in class, at soccer games, at home, almost anywhere and anytime. I straight up played Hungry Hungry Hippo on my fingers. I have a strong immune system from all the fingernail germs I consumed throughout the years.

Despite my elementary traumas, fears, and desire to be accepted, my parents loved me deeply. They sacrificed much to provide for our family. My dad worked hard to give our family the best life possible. My parents were involved in our sporting events, they took us on family vacations, camping trips, fishing trips, and many other wonderful adventures.

My dad has a big heart. I love him very much and I respect him. But we lacked deep intimacy as father and son. As a young boy, I desired to feel safe and secure. But because my dad didn't know Jesus, he didn't know true intimacy. How then could he have given me what he didn't have?

CHAPTER FOUR

Exploring and Wandering

MY INSECURITIES FOLLOWED me into middle school. By then I completed the foundation of my spiritual Alcatraz. I moved on to reinforce the walls and extend the labyrinth of the corridors. I built many new prison cells and established a routine for visiting them.

I disliked sixth through eighth grade. I attended Highlands Middle School through second semester of eighth grade. New faces, an unfamiliar school, and older kids intimidated me. Even the bus stop instilled hesitancy and anxiety.

I sat at the front of the bus. Only the popular and cool kids sat in the back. Feeling trapped, I stared out the window and avoided eye contact. Sometimes kids behind me threw things at the back of my head and laughed at me. I avoided interaction. I pretended nothing happened and allowed the behavior to perpetuate.

Off the bus and in school presented uncharted territory. Many things affected and shaped my experiences. Music played a significant role. The eighties produced some of the greatest music ever.

I knew most of the popular songs from the major artists and bands. I sang to Michael Jackson, Prince, Madonna, Run D.M.C., Cyndi Lauper, Pat Benatar, Bon Jovi, and Guns N' Roses. MTV heavily influenced how I talked, acted, and dressed. I panicked if I forgot to wear my Swatch Watch.

I taught myself to breakdance. I breakdanced in the street, at playgrounds and roller skating rinks. A flat piece of cardboard provided a mobile dance floor. I bought a pair of red parachute pants like Michael Jackson wore on his "Thriller" video. I think I wore them for 363 ½ days one year.

Breakdancing provided a wonderful outlet for me. It allowed me to express myself and fit in with the older kids. I used breakdancing to show off and prove myself to others. Music and breakdancing helped elevate my likeable and popular status.

I figured my breakdancing skills would carry over to social dances too. Not so. Social dances terrified me. I attended my first sock hop dance in eighth grade. Girls lined up on one side of the dance floor. Boys lined up on the other side. A teacher announced for the girls to pick a partner. Girls with crushes on the same boy sparked dramatic arguments.

The environment revealed the depths of my timidity. I avoided eye contact hoping not to be noticed or picked. A girl just as terrified as me picked me last. I didn't attend middle school dances again.

Besides listening to music and dancing, God gifted me with musical talent. I played the piano, but I didn't identify it as talent. I competed in various talent shows. I won a few. Fear of failure and embarrassment predisposed me to lose before the contest began. I didn't celebrate my wins but punished my losses. I assaulted my confidence with phrases like, *See, I told you, you are worthless. You suck. You embarrassed yourself on stage.*

Most talent shows and recitals handed out placement ribbons. I treated all ribbons except first place like a piece of garbage. I would not accept less than first place. I constructed a framework for value and worth through performance and perfection.

I played piano for the middle school orchestra. But cool kids didn't join an orchestra or band. Only nerds, geeks, low lives, and hermits did. I didn't want to be one of those labels.

In eighth grade our orchestra class went to a major event to compete against other schools. I stepped out of my comfort zone and sat in the last row of the bus. To show off, I decided to sing a song by the group 2 Live Crew, a group known for crude and perverse sexual lyrics.

The other kids laughed and smirked. Some laughed with me. Some laughed at me because of my naivete. The attention exhilarated me. Cheers fueled on more brazen and defiant singing. In the end my orchestra teacher scolded me over the bus PA system.

Beyond musical talent, God also gifted me with athletic ability. I learned the basic soccer skills in grade school. By age twelve my soccer skills increased and people noticed. But Highlands Middle School didn't have a reputation for producing the David Beckhams of the world. On a team of mediocre players, I loved being the best player.

With the spotlight on me I exuded confidence and cockiness. I soaked up the applause and cheers for me at games. I did ridiculous things like bicycle kicks in the middle of the field. I only did them to hear players "ooh" and "aah." The attention and focus made me feel valuable. I continued to hone my soccer abilities.

I dabbled in a couple other sports too. I determined I could have the same swagger as a wrestler. But nobody "oohed" and "aahedd" when I joined the eighty-pound weight class in eighth grade. I entered a tournament in Moses Lake, Washington.

Somehow in my mind I equated my wrestling skills to my soccer skills. I won a few matches and made it to the middle round. I wrestled against the best wrestler in the state. I got owned. In a matter of seconds my back met the mat. I cried, gave up, and let him pin me. Defeat consumed my thoughts. I quit wrestling afterwards.

I didn't understand why I weighed only eighty pounds. Many other guys were over a hundred pounds and taller. They filled out, grew a few inches, and had deeper voices. The bigger guys hit puberty at twelve and thirteen. Puberty came late for me. I didn't hit puberty until almost fifteen. I considered my slow physical development a handicap.

My small size didn't matter on the ski slopes. I learned to snow ski and bought season passes to Ski Bluewood in Oregon. I sensed God's familiar presence in the peace I found on the slopes. My heart fluttered in how He gently wooed and called to me.

But skiing served a darker purpose too. Alone in a tree run I fantasized *What if I skied passed the out of bounds marker to a place where nobody could find me? or What if I just disappeared in the mountains and let the snow bury me?*

The bus ride home from the mountain provided little comfort. The teenagers sat in the back and drank booze. They acted crude and belligerent. On a few occasions, a couple performed oral sex on each other. Being exposed to vulgar behavior on a regular basis distorted my outlook.

Other activities besides, sports, music, and hobbies influenced me. Around seventh grade I discovered the Ouija board. The mysticism of it fascinated me. I hid in a room for hours with friends and played the Ouija board. We met different spirits and learned their names. I knew which ones were friendly and which ones weren't. We sought guidance, direction, and affirmation from the Ouija board.

I considered the Ouija board fun and harmless. I didn't realize the darkness I exposed myself to. Addicted, days went by seeking my next Ouija board fix. My friends and I even dabbled in performing séances with candles. I watched the movie *Witchboard* when it came out.

Even school projects imprinted moments of hardship in my mind. Of all my middle school classes, I enjoyed science the most.

I participated in a contest to build the strongest bridge made out of balsa wood. I teamed up with my dad over a weekend. We bought materials, planned the structure and built the support beams. I radiated with joy. I wanted my dad to be proud of me.

All the parents and students gathered together in the school cafeteria on the day of the contest. The science teacher displayed all the bridges on the stage. Everyone applauded their marvelous creations. One by one the teacher tied a weight to a string and hung it from the bottom of a bridge. Everyone passed the first round. But as he added more weight, bridges collapsed and snapped.

Parents consoled the kids whose bridges collapsed. I stayed in the contest round after round until three bridges remained. My bridge went first. The extra weight bent it to almost breaking point. I knew my bridge wouldn't survive another round. I hoped the other bridges would break that round. They didn't.

I won third place. My dad congratulated me and encouraged me. But my heart hurt. In my mind I let him down. I wanted to brag about my dad. The smartest and best dad in the world. I didn't celebrate my accomplishment. I failed my dad. The weight of disappointment turned joys into sorrows. By the middle of my eighth grade year I made a few steps up the social ladder. I overcame my sixth grade skittishness. But my whole world changed in December of 1988 when our family moved from Kennewick to Richland, Washington.

Devastated, I wanted to wake up from the nightmare. I detested the thought of another family moving into *my* house. I didn't want anyone to make memories or have fun in my house. The hint of a strange kid in my bedroom repulsed me. I built my hiding place and fortress of solitude there. All others trespassed.

I attended my last day at Highlands Middle School on a Friday. I cried on the walk home from the bus stop. I stopped several times and looked back. Troubled, my parents tried to comfort me. My view of friendships and "good things" in life changed.

I convinced myself good things would always come to an end. I challenged what I let into my heart. Why get close to someone or something? In the end I'd be abandoned.

On Monday I began the second semester at Carmichael Middle School in Richland. Carmichael seemed like a foreign land. The smells, sounds, and hallways were unfamiliar. For the first couple weeks I spoke only when spoken to. I counted the hours and minutes until the last bell rang.

I embarrassed myself three weeks into English class. My teacher told a story about a mother whose young son died. She purchased a grave lot with a small, plain headstone. A fancier marble headstone lay next to it. The teacher asked the class why the mom only got her son a small, plain headstone. I raised my hand for the first time in class. Full of confidence I said, "Because she didn't love him?"

The entire class gasped and rebuked me with disgust. "No, it's because she didn't have any money." I wanted to teleport away to Mars. My answer made sense to me. I didn't love myself. I wanted to quit Carmichael Middle School after class.

New friends did not come easily for me. I hung out with kids the rest of the school deemed as vagrants and social outcasts—not because I showcased a good heart or compassion for them, I wanted to fit in.

Spanish class afforded me an opportunity to step up. At first, I behaved and pretended to be a good student, until I realized the students ran the class. The students disrespected the teacher. She carried no authority with zero disciplinary actions or consequences.

One student brought a glass-vile stink bomb to class. He looked at me and said, "Hey Bill, watch this." He threw the vile on the floor underneath the teacher's desk. The vile shattered. The stench of rotten eggs choked the air in the room. The class laughed and covered their noses. I couldn't believe what happened. My mouth foamed at the chance to participate.

I brought a box of grape Nerds candy to class. I didn't know what to do with them. But I knew I wouldn't eat them. The teacher wrote on the chalkboard and my creative juices flowed. I filled my hands up with Nerds. I hurled the Nerds towards the chalkboard. They made a loud rain stick sound as they peppered the chalkboard. Grape Nerds landed in her hair, on the chalkboard rail, and rolled on the floor.

At first, I thought, *What did I just do? I am so busted.* I didn't receive a prompt escort to the principal's office. Instead, my teacher picked up one of the Nerds and smelled it. Her reaction triggered an eruption of laughter. After class I received many accolades and congratulations for my accomplishment. I continued similar types of shenanigans in her class. I associated value with class disruption.

But my classroom antics didn't produce real friends. I returned to my old Kennewick friends in the summer between middle school and high school. I made little effort to create new relationships or friendships in Richland. I dared not betray my Kennewick friends.

My Kennewick friends introduced me to alcohol. I tasted my first alcoholic drink at age thirteen. My friend's older brother invited people over to his house for a party. Teenage girls in bikinis drank from a keg and swam in the pool. The desire to impress the big kids overpowered my meek state of mind. I acted tough and told jokes. But I didn't participate in the extracurricular activities. Until the moment my friend handed me a red keg cup. "Here. Drink this beer."

"What will it do to me?"

"Don't worry, it will be awesome. You will feel happy."

Ill-equipped to say no, I pounded the entire cup. The beer stunk and disgusted me. At the time, I stood about five feet tall and weighed less than one hundred pounds. The cup of beer should have wasted me, but didn't.

I acted silly and hyper in front of my friend. I pretended to be drunk. But I wasn't. I believe God protected me from the effects of the alcohol.

Summer came to a close. In August I attended a week-long soccer camp at Whidbey Island. Boys and girls of varied skill levels attended. The coaching staff noticed my skills from day one. By the end of the week I established a decent reputation in the camp.

We stayed in old military barracks. The coaches required all players to shower. An open bathroom with no partitions offered zero privacy. I wanted to quit soccer camp to avoid the showers. A few cocky players showered first. They cracked jokes and bragged about themselves.

I stalled and hid. I wanted to shower in my shorts. The coaches didn't allow me. Sick to my stomach, I undressed. I drowned in shame and inadequacy. I remained paranoid about the guys' stares and jokes the rest of the camp.

A talent show capped off the last night of camp. Players broke up into groups of six or seven. Each group performed an act or skit on a stage. Wounded from the shower experience, I refused to participate. A dance followed the talent show. I declined the dance as well.

Surprised by my decision, one of the guys said, "Whoa, I thought for sure you would dance. You are the best soccer player here and most popular with the coaches. How can you be so good at soccer, crack so many jokes, but be afraid to dance?"

My middle school years ended in disappointment.

CHAPTER FIVE

Still Worthless

I HAVE TRIED to forget most of my freshman year at Richland High School. Another strange school with unfamiliar faces restarted the cycle of fear and rejection. I scurried around the hallways like a little mouse.

Uncomfortable and out of place, I expended little energy towards making new friends. I refused to stop living in my past. I couldn't let go of my Kennewick house, my Kennewick friends, my Kennewick life.

Thankfully, soccer remained constant in my life. My calendar revolved around soccer for four years in high school. Soccer balanced me and allowed me to showcase my athletic skills. Looking back, I realize the health benefits, leadership skills, and social skills I gained. I grasped fundamentals, strategy, and tactics with ease.

Richland's soccer program produced strong teams. My Brazilian coach trained our team like we were professionals. I started the majority of the varsity games throughout my high school career. My team advanced to the playoffs all four years. We also placed second and third in the state playoffs.

In summer and fall I played on Premier 1 teams. I played in the Washington Olympic Development Program (ODP) my junior and senior years. By age nineteen I had played four years of varsity soccer, Premier 1, Washington ODP, and tournaments in various countries in Europe. Few teenagers enjoyed those opportunities.

But I didn't earn any of them on my own. God gifted me with the talent and opportunities. I rejected my gifts and denied my abilities.

My Premier 1 coach approached me during a practice. "You know," he said, "you are one of the best all-around players I have ever seen." A desirable compliment from one of the most well-known and respected coaches in the soccer community.

I responded without appreciation or gratitude. "No. I am not. I suck."

He asked what college I wanted to play for.

"I am not interested in playing soccer in college, I am done with soccer."

My lack of interest did not reflect the opportunities offered to me. University of California Santa Barbara, the United States Naval Academy in Annapolis, Maryland, and Whitworth University in Spokane, Washington offered various scholarships.

The coach for Whitworth invited me to come to the campus for a tour and discuss playing for the team. I refused in a not-so-polite manner. I realize now the wasted opportunity.

Stubborn and selfish, I couldn't see the potential my coaches saw. I admit, I lavished in momentary celebrations from teammates and fans when I performed well. I enjoyed high fives and compliments for great plays. But all the compliments in the world were no match against the voice of *I am still not good enough.*

I punished myself for minor mistakes—simple things like a missed trap or inaccurate pass. In extreme cases I kicked the ball down the field to draw attention away from me. I turned my back towards the fans and cried.

I did have a life outside of soccer. Other activities occupied my time. As a freshman I landed my first job—as a busboy at the country club near where we lived—and worked there until I graduated from high school. I started at $2.21 an hour.

Girls weren't quite on my radar yet. But I met two girls from a different school my freshman summer. After a couple months as friends I snuck out a few times at night with one of them. We looked for trouble. One time, we tagged a car with soap and wrapped it in toilet paper. I ignored the internal alarms warning me of wrongdoing. But I did what she wanted to impress her.

I went to her house one Saturday night to watch a movie. I sat on the couch next to her. She attempted to touch my leg and I pretended not to notice. After several failed attempts, she went into the bathroom.

When she returned she handed me a note: "Wait until we are alone and then we can have sex." A few moments later I faked an upset stomach and left. Appalled at my blatant rejection, she didn't want to hang out with me after that. Not a good way to end my freshman summer.

My sophomore year began how my freshman year ended. Inadequacy, rejection, and worthlessness escorted me to my sophomore year. Our PE teacher announced mandatory showers for the boys. I relived the same shower fears from the Whidbey Island soccer camp. The locker room contained a handful of poles with multiple shower spouts per pole. The boys showered in close proximity to each other.

The open space prevented anyone from hiding. Exposed and vulnerable, I cowered into the showers. The PE teacher stood at the shower exit and handed out towels. I hung my head in shame.

Before I conceded high school as a total loss, my sixteenth birthday arrived. My Kennewick friends and a few Richland friends attended my party. I opened presents around my parents' huge dining table. I received a football, a cool shirt, and a couple hip-hop tapes. I wanted all those things but couldn't wait to see what my parents bought me.

I tore into the wrapping paper to find a rainbow-colored backpack. My friends tried to contain their laughter. We thought my parents played a funny joke. "Oh," I said. "I know, the real surprise is stuffed inside the backpack." I reached into the pocket hoping to find a wad of Benjamins or something spectacular. Instead, I pulled out two packets of grape-flavored Big League Chew shredded bubble gum.

Certain I missed something; I dug deeper. Seeing the frustrated look on my face, my friends erupted in laughter. I looked past my parent's genuine intention and only felt cheated.

I did not allow the momentous occasion to be ruined by a rainbow-colored backpack. I attempted to redeem myself with an act of toughness. I ordered everyone downstairs and said, "Hey, anyone want to take a shot of hard alcohol with me?" I reacted spontaneously. I poured alcohol into a shot glass I snuck from my parent's liquor cabinet.

I slammed it and waited for praise and accolades from my friends. They shook their heads in disbelief. In addition to their lame response, I felt no physical effects from the alcohol. I believe God protected me from the effects again.

The real prize of my sixteenth birthday didn't reside in presents. Above all gifts, I wanted a driver's license. I passed my written and practical exams with a score of ninety-two. My driver's license opened up a realm of new possibilities for me.

I drove a 1979 El Camino with faded copper-colored paint and a three-speed stick shift. If you drove a car you were required to have a boomin' system. I saved up enough money and installed a CD player, an amp, and my brother's twelve-inch home tower speakers.

I purchased my first three CDs: DJ Quik, AC/DC, and Geto Boys. At sixteen I embraced the profound effect of music on my mind. Different lyrics, beats, and sound effects invoked various reactions from me. I enjoyed listening to music for the sake of music. But certain songs triggered intense emotional responses.

I jammed out to hip-hop and heavy metal most often. I played artists like NWA, Ice Cube, and Metallica. Certain songs dragged me into an emotional abyss. Almost hypnotized, my eyes glazed over song after song. On many occasions, I arrived at my home or destination with no recollection of the commute.

Hip-hop raised my awareness of racism and prejudice. Around March of my sophomore year, I golfed more frequently. The majority of members at my parents' country club were over fifty-five, Caucasian, and wealthy. As I was a brown-skinned teenager, people could easily spot me. I set up a tee time with two of my friends to play a round of golf.

We made our way towards the first hole. The golf pro and some of his friends confronted us. I gave him my membership number and last name. In a demeaning and condescending tone, he insisted I could not play.

I sprinted to my house to get my driver's license. While away, my friends said the golf pro and his friends laughed, joked, and uttered racial slurs. When I returned, I stared the golf pro in the eyes. "Here's my driver's license with the last name Ker." My mom gave him a piece of her mind too.

I experienced my first blatant and personal racist attack that day. As a result, I developed a heightened sensitivity towards racism.

Summer arrived and I had survived two years of high school. Summer marked the transition period to upper classman. I wanted to get serious about drinking to enhance my popularity.

One day my friend invited me to stay the night. I again snuck alcohol from my parent's liquor cabinet. I poured several different kinds of liquor into a large cup. I didn't know any specific drink recipes. The concoction smelled wretched. I didn't care.

I hurried to my friend's house. We were alone and drunk within a few minutes. We ate pastrami sandwiches, jumped on his couch, and acted juvenile. About an hour later the room spun and

I vomited in the toilet. The next day I understood the meaning of a hangover.

The alcohol elicited intense physiological and emotional responses. The toxic mixture of my sorrow and alcohol deepened the recesses of my mind. I held a ribbon-cutting ceremony for a brand-new section of my spiritual Alcatraz.

I believe God protected me from the effects of alcohol the previous two times. The desire to get drunk wasn't in my heart. But my sophomore summer changed that. Alcohol became entwined with my life.

CHAPTER SIX

Out of Control

B Y THE TIME my junior year started, I had accumulated a decent amount of friends and acquaintances. I achieved *some* status but wanted more.

Richland High School gained a reputation for being a "hick" school. The school upheld its stereotype of 4 × 4s, rear window gun racks, and country music. I avoided flannel and country music.

Music continued to inspire me to express myself. I also used it to gain approval and value from people. The people I hung out with determined what music I played. One day I listened to Led Zeppelin, Ozzy Osbourne, Nirvana, and the next day Color Me Badd, Madonna, and Tupac.

Hip-hop molded my identity. I adopted the culture and adapted my life to it. I wanted to be black. I wanted to be tough. I wanted people to respect me. I tried to act thug and gangsta. I hid my brokenness and pretended to be someone and something else.

I upgraded my car from the El Camino to a blue 1989 Chevy S-10. I added tinted windows, lowered it, and installed a powerful stereo system. I bumped the bass everywhere I went. Unashamed, I shouted out the violent and vulgar lyrics degrading women.

I displayed my affinity for rap culture. For several weeks I begged my parents to let me get a Raiders coat. They hesitated due to the image it portrayed. Eventually my parents caved. I dressed in my Oakland Raiders hat and coat most of the time. But I wasn't a fan and didn't know anyone on the team.

I bragged about guns even though I didn't own one. For thirteen weeks I wore a cast on my right leg from a soccer injury. The cast stretched from my toes to my hip. I inscribed various gang graffiti markings on it.

I confronted the gangsta image in my high school library. A friend of mine brought a loaded .357 Magnum to school. I met up with him in the library where he volunteered.

"Hey, check this out." He lifted his shirt and revealed the nickel plated gun. I tried to act cool. "Word 'em up homie. That's gangsta."

But the seriousness of the situation petrified me. My heart raced. I didn't want to get caught. I wasn't prepared to live the life of a thug.

The façade of the truck, Raiders' apparel and hip hop image concealed my anguish. I used them to maintain a false sense of security and identity. I needed artificial realities to give me purpose.

I found other ways to gain acceptance. High school culture exuded pressure to have a girlfriend or to "have girls." A male gained status and popularity by sleeping around. I fabricated stories of girls I slept with. Women carried the label of "slut" while guys boasted the label of "champion."

I wanted to be a champion. At parties I listened to my friends and other guys brag about who they slept with. I wanted to brag about women I slept with too. I dreamt up elaborate sex stories with random women at different parties. When asked for their names I said, "Oh you wouldn't know her. She doesn't go to this school or live around here."

I manufactured make-believe women who never existed. I beamed with pride to the cheers and high fives from my friends. Nobody knew my virgin status. But their reactions fueled my confidence. My lies perpetuated through my junior and senior years.

Even my two real girlfriends didn't know my secret. Both girls were attractive, outgoing, and personable. I bought them gifts and went on romantic dates. We talked on the phone and wrote notes to each other. I reciprocated attention and affection.

Despite my attraction, I broke up with them after a few months. I blamed my own insecurities and lack of confidence. I genuinely desired friendship, companionship and affection with a girl. But I denied girls access to my heart. I broke their hearts because of my broken mind.

My broken mind stunted growth in relationships at Richland. I refused to give up living in my past. I remained loyal to my Kennewick friends. At times I resented Richland. I overreacted during a party my Richland friend hosted.

A couple hours and several drinks into the party, my friend swiped my Raiders hat. He hid it and wouldn't give it back. He laughed and teased for fun. But I blew up at his harmless joke. I ran my mouth off about how much Richland sucked. I yelled out my resentment for moving to Richland. "I am going to transfer back to Kennewick."

Many people at the party pulled me aside. "Bill, chill out, settle down. You are talking crazy right now." I didn't stop. I slammed the door on my way out of the apartment. I screamed obscenities about Richland as I walked down the sidewalk.

The buildup of years of frustration erupted over a stupid Raiders hat. I lived in the past and denied the future. The turmoil between the two manifested at the party. By Monday morning when I returned to school, I regretted spouting off. Some of my closer friends let me know just how belligerent I acted.

I struggled to deal with my anxieties and vulnerabilities. I thought I found solace in alcohol and parties. I prided myself on the bridge I built between my Kennewick and Richland friends. The friends whom I considered closer than brothers I brought together and enjoyed the best of both worlds. My friends and I spent most of our weekends behind the Horse Heaven Hills and on the banks of the Yakima River.

We burned wood pallets on a bonfire and bumped music. Each night started off the same. The boys drank forty-ounce bottles of malt liquor and the girls drank wine coolers.

I laughed and sang along to different songs. But, the more I drank, the deeper I dove into the recesses of my mind. Once I reached a certain level my demeanor changed. The music started out upbeat and energetic. Then I switched it to melancholy to match my mood. A song like "It's So Hard to Say Goodbye to Yesterday" by Boyz II Men changed the atmosphere of the party.

My shoulders and posture slumped. My body language communicated my despondency. At random moments I wandered off into the trees. Or I walked away into the darkness to be alone. Thoughts of suicide flashed in and out of my mind.

I robed myself with worthlessness and wallowed in my misery. I repeated the weekend cycle. I drank, listened to sad songs, and expressed my sorrow. My self-worth deteriorated.

Low self-worth justified risky and dangerous behavior. Most times, nobody volunteered to be a designated driver on the weekends. A lack of a sober driver didn't deter me. Many times I cruised the main streets while I drank a forty ounce.

I dismissed the dangers of driving while under the influence. I scoffed at the potential to get a DUI. With no hope in my heart, I worried little about my irresponsible decisions. Consequences didn't concern me. I figured, if I ended up hurt or dead who cares?

Drinking and partying became the fabric of my life. I built a reputation and created a culture that exalted weekend mischief. Each year the junior and senior class held a secret "sleep out" the last week of school. It always fell on a weeknight.

I knew I would be a perfect fit and a star of the party. I asked my parents for permission to go. I resented their decision to not allow me.

I woke up infuriated the morning after the sleep out. In defiance I snuck four or five shots of alcohol into a soccer water jug. The students who attended the sleep out were tired and hung over. I asked them to describe the night to me. "It was so fun. You totally missed out and should have been there."

Those comments stoked my fire of anger and resentment. I went to lunch with two of my close friends off campus. I expressed my discontent and held the jug to my mouth.

"You are going to drink that now?" they said.

"Hell yah." I slammed the two or three gulps of alcohol. Drunk after a few minutes, we headed back to school.

Lit up, I ran my mouth during fourth, fifth, and sixth periods. I lunged into chemistry class and hugged my teacher. Startled, he said, "Whoa Bill. Why are you acting so strange?" The class exploded in laughter. How I didn't get caught remains a mystery.

Being drunk in school catapulted my reputation to a new level. The risk, the students' reactions, and my ego made me feel valued and popular.

But I didn't only seek affirmation and reputation through alcohol. I needed it to numb my pain. I never used hard-core drugs like cocaine, heroin, meth and others. I feared them. But I experimented with Robitussin.

I supposed Robitussin might medicate my pain like alcohol did. I drank two bottles of it on two separate occasions. Both times wrecked me. I hallucinated and vomited violently.

Cough medicine didn't heal my wounds. But I continued the search for the one thing to make me feel loved.

CHAPTER SEVEN

Alcohol Daze

THE SUMMER BEFORE my senior year, I traveled to Europe to play soccer tournaments. For most, going to Europe, let alone playing soccer, is a once-in-a-lifetime opportunity. I held a more selfish view of the trip: get drunk and be independent.

Our team stayed in England for about a week. First, we visited London near Wembley Stadium. I brought my hip-hop identity with me. I wore my Raiders' hat with a white bandana underneath. I wanted to make a statement to the Londoners. But the mix of races and dense population camouflaged my presence. Because of a jam-packed schedule, I didn't have many opportunities to drink.

Next we stayed in Stoke-on-Trent with host families. The son in my host family played soccer for a local team. I bonded with the family and their grandparents. The family treated me well and showed me around the city. I pierced both ears in a local beauty salon. Another piece of façade to mask my anguish.

On the second night of my stay, I persuaded the host family's son to take me to a pub. The experience fascinated me. Locals sat around me at a table and I told stories about American culture. Someone bought me a Guinness. I gagged when I took a sip. A few laughed at my reaction, others seemed insulted. I ordered vodka instead. The unusual request surprised some.

I embellished half the stories about my life in America. Intrigued and with eyes fixed on me, I fed the local's desire for more. After my fifth or sixth shot one guy said, "Whoa, slow down Bill. You are drinking that vodka like water." My thirst for vodka seemed abnormal to him. For me, I sometimes drank vodka from the bottle in America.

The next day I met the sister of a player on the local team. To me she stepped out of the pages of a beauty magazine. Yes, the "love at first sight" cliché is true. But I asked myself, *How could someone like her be interested in someone like me?* I poured my heart out to her the rest of the trip. My efforts were futile.

I fooled myself. Feelings of not good enough, not big enough, not strong enough neutralized my affection. I chalked her up to an unrealistic dream. For six months I sulked over an imaginary relationship that never existed.

My soccer team lost in the quarter finals of the tournament. By the last night in England I regarded my host family as extended family. Our team and host families gathered at a local pub. We shed tears and said goodbyes. Depressed and distraught, I drank $60 worth of drinks in a few minutes.

I scolded myself. I had become too attached to my host family and the girl I liked. I said, *See what happens when you let people get too close? You just end up getting hurt.* Wounded, I hardened my heart.

Our team stayed in Holland and Germany the remaining two weeks of the trip. We placed second in the tournament in Holland. We won our friendly match in Germany. We experienced many amazing things in the two countries, visited many historic parts of the cities, and also toured the Rhine River on a boat.

However, my selfish agenda remained the same—get drunk and be independent. I disregarded the privilege of learning about the culture and history of the two countries. Instead, I convinced my teammates to play hours of blackjack for quarters. I dealt and the majority of the time I won. My winnings supplied the means to by alcohol.

The overall trip left an indelible print in my mind and memories. I carried my confused identity into my senior year. I still wore my Raiders' gear, blasted hip-hop music and imitated a gangsta façade. But my unquenchable need for more identity persisted.

Jewelry appeared to be a suitable addition. I adorned myself with various kinds. I adopted the nickname "Gypsy" because of the many earrings, necklaces, rings and bracelets I wore. These provided additional covers to hide under.

I switched up my style of clothing to keep up the momentum of disguise. I dressed in a silk shirt one day and the next day I sported flannel. Yes, I conceded and wore flannel. I collected various kinds of cologne. Certain fragrances triggered powerful memories. I loved girls' reactions when they hugged me. My ponytail-length hair also provided a sense of concealment and comfort. I beamed when girls cooed over my soft hair.

Nevertheless, I panicked if I lost my Raiders' hat or jewelry. On the rare occasion I forgot something, I turned around halfway to school to get it. I didn't risk going through a school day bare and exposed.

Time passed and the accumulation of hurt became difficult to suppress. Poetry and short stories provided additional means to express my turmoil. They shared common themes laced with sorrow and despondency. I dedicated love poems to a woman I made up in my mind. I fantasized and dreamt of being with a girl who could love me, despite me.

I often shared my poems with girls I had non-romantic friendships with. Their adoring responses affirmed me. We partied together, confided in each other, and shared mutual interests. Even their boyfriends didn't feel threatened or uncomfortable by me. Those friendships meant the world to me.

But I still craved more attention from girls to feel loved. Fueled by poor decisions made while drunk, I broke the trust of genuine friendships. I crossed the line when I made advances on a few of my female friends.

I ruined a relationship with a couple loyal to me. I asked one of the girls for permission to kiss her at a party. Somehow, her boyfriend found out. He showed up at my house a few days later. "You know why I am here. The only reason why I am not punching you in the face right now is because we used to be such good friends."

I wondered why I jeopardized friendships to feel loved. What triggered my desperation for love and attention?

One Saturday afternoon I stood in the kitchen with my mom as we watched a TV show. The segment focused on adopted kids who met their biological parents for the first time. The biological parents explained why they made the decision to adopt. Some shared reasons with good intentions and others admitted abandonment. My mom looked at me with tears in her eyes. "Bill, you know, I hope you don't think your parents put you up for adoption because they didn't want you."

For eighteen years I acted indifferent towards my adoption. But her comment forced me to face my identity crisis. Over the next several days I brawled with it. My biological mom was Filipina and my biological dad was Caucasian. My skin was brown. But I didn't know the Filipino culture or language.

Lost in cultural confusion, I tried to latch onto other races. I imitated my Hispanic and black friends. I tried to escape my own skin. I didn't see myself as unique or special and was unaware at the time that abandonment and rejection had rooted in my mind.

I experienced God's love repeatedly. He pursued me but I pushed Him away. *No, Jesus, you cannot love me. Let me keep this sorrow. I deserve this. I don't deserve your love. I cannot allow you to love me.* But I desperately wanted to receive His love. I didn't know how.

I hoped to find a glimmer of love at homecoming and prom. Disillusioned from my past, I convinced my Richland date to go with me to Kennewick's homecoming. We went together with my best friend from Kennewick and his Richland date.

We arrived at the dance and I pranced around like I owned the place. I wanted to be more than friends with my date. I wanted to impress her. But I didn't receive the accolades I hoped for. Of the handful of people I knew, a few said, "Whoa, what are you doing at *our* homecoming?" Treated like an outsider and my date unimpressed, the night ended in anticlimactic fashion. Our potential romantic future faded.

I vowed redemption at prom on my home turf. I asked my friend's sister to prom. I also wanted to be more than friends with her. With my black hair slicked back and in a silver tux, I looked like a mobster wannabe. My date stole the show in an elegant white dress. She received numerous compliments while I received sneers and snickers.

I learned from my homecoming mistakes. For several hours I didn't make a fool of myself. I respected her and acted semi-mature. We ate dinner at a popular restaurant with many others from prom. After we finished we walked towards the exit. My date was in front of me when we approached a set of four wooden stairs. She slipped and fell down the steps. In the process she rolled her ankle.

People within visual distance gasped. Shocked, I paused at the top of the steps. "Are you okay?" Several other guys from surrounding tables arose to her aid. Several of her friends also rushed to her—before I could reach her. I helped her limp out of the restaurant. Several witnesses to the incident glared at me. Someone shouted, "Way to go Bill you just left her there."

The incident haunted me the rest of the night. I embarrassed my date and made a fool of myself. I recited in my mind, *See, you are a mistake. No girl wants to be with you.*

I swore an oath not to end my senior year on my prom disaster note. I wanted to memorialize my reputation before graduation. I needed to prove I accomplished something besides mistakes the last four years. In the final month before graduation, some of the seniors planned the senior sleep out. I joined in.

I decided to make a giant spodie. I prepared for a couple of weeks. I borrowed and collected hundreds of dollars. I bought fruit, the fruit punch, the liquor, and a thirty-two-gallon garbage can. I persuaded my friend to tell his mom to lie to my mom. I scripted the entire conversation. She told my mom over the phone that several seniors would sleep in the basement and watch movies.

The seniors met in a parking lot the day of the sleep out. I hauled two coolers full of hard alcohol and fruit in the back of my truck. The popular guys looked at me and said, "Where do you want to go, you are the one with the majority of the alcohol." A jolt of power surged through my veins. The senior sleep out location rested on my shoulders.

I pronounced a popular spot behind the Horse Heaven Hills in Richland. A half-mile-long caravan of vehicles headed out. We arrived and vehicles scattered throughout the sagebrush and cheat grass. I filled up the new thirty-two-gallon garbage can with the two coolers of alcohol, fruit and seventeen gallons of fruit punch.

People watched with amazement. They hovered around and jockeyed for position in line. I opened the spodie at $5 a cup and people swarmed. People were buzzed before those in the back of line even got a cup. I received many high fives and compliments on the success of the spodie. I basked in the fame. I stood at the pinnacle of my popularity. I thought my achievement would give me a lifetime of value and bragging rights.

But I experienced the opposite feeling. I wandered off several feet from the crowd. I observed everyone laughing and having a good time. I realized the hole inside my heart felt as empty as before I created the spodie.

About 2:00 a.m., twenty or thirty drunken seniors drove back to the high school. We crashed on campus in the grassy courtyard area. I lay in my sleeping bag and a few guys took off with my truck. Together with several other guys, they drove around the city and stole lawn ornaments. They transported them back to the courtyard in the high school.

The guys even managed to acquire a phone booth from a local convenience store. The next morning the principal and faculty arrived. They found the courtyard decorated with lawn ornaments and passed out senior classmen. The police arrived an hour later along with a big truck. Several students delivered the stolen materials back to the owners.

In the end, I gained a reputation and status. Gossip about the sleep out lasted through graduation. But my lust for acceptance bypassed all common sense and danger. I didn't contemplate the stain on the high school's reputation. I didn't consider the possibility of students going to jail. I didn't realize a parent could have lost a son or daughter in a DUI.

Graduation day arrived. I gazed at my fellow classmates during rehearsal in the gym. I loved some students like brothers and sisters. Others I barely knew. Everyone expressed various emotional responses.

The graduation ceremony hit me like a freight train. I tried to comprehend the past eighteen years of my life. I sat about ten rows back from the stage in the aisle next to the walkway. After everyone received their diplomas the principle announced we graduated. Before the entire senior class reacted, I leapt up. With arms held high I shouted at the top of my lungs.

A photographer from the local newspaper ran over to me and snapped a few photos. My response triggered the rest of the senior class to stand and shout. We removed our graduation caps and launched them into the air.

The next morning my parents and grandma dropped a stack of newspapers at the foot of my bed. The front page photo showed the moment I leaped up and shouted at the graduation ceremony. I yearned for the photo to signify the sum total of my value and worth. To me, it was a trophy I idolized. Proof of the blood, sweat, and tears I invested to ascend to the highest level of popularity.

Still shattered and broken inside, I recognized the photo wasn't my savior. The photo and what it represented didn't fill the void, provide hope, or give me purpose.

CHAPTER EIGHT

Wild About Women

I PRESSED ON from graduation. My party routine continued through the summer before college. Around July I briefly dated a girl from Kennewick. We didn't know each other well and the relationship didn't develop into much. However, we hung out together at parties. I didn't know the local town thug used to be her boyfriend.

One Saturday night I met up with friends at a popular Taco Bell that was packed with standing room only. We ordered and I chatted with people sitting at a table. Suddenly, a piece of taco hit my shoulder. I laughed and assumed one of my friends threw it. Then two more pieces of taco hit my shoulder. I turned around. Three guys faced me about five feet away. The ex-boyfriend thug without a shirt on stood among them.

I walked up to him. "What's this about? Is this about her?"

"What about her?"

"I am not interested in squabin' with you."

I turned to walk back to my friends. When I did, he sucker punched me in the side of my head, knocking off my hat. I stepped towards him to retaliate. My friends blocked me, "Stop, you are bleeding."

A mass of people ran for the door. The three guys ducked out and disappeared into the crowd. The punch split open my right eyebrow. My friend drove me to the emergency room and I received seven stitches. People later told me he hit me with brass knuckles.

Word spread about the fight. I learned I wasn't his only victim. He apparently enjoyed beating up on people. His reputation worried me.

Paranoid and consumed with fear, I avoided public places. The rest of the summer I walked around with one eye over my shoulder. I saw him one other time but from a long distance. I remained fearful to go out in public in the Tri-Cities for a couple years.

But the incident didn't damper my excitement for college. I turned down the colleges who offered me soccer scholarships. I chose to attend Eastern Washington University in Cheney, Washington. Voracious to be independent, I left home one full week before classes began.

I shared a dorm room with one of my closest friends from Kennewick. Upon arrival, we hooked up the stereo, opened our door and bumped hip-hop music. I wanted first thing to establish my identity and presence.

We lived on a co-ed floor and became friends with several people. We recruited a twenty-one-year-old Japanese exchange student to be our alcohol supplier. I used money set aside for school supplies and books to buy alcohol. We drank each night before the first day of class began.

Liberated and on my own, I thrived and I adjusted to the unfamiliar faces and places of the university. Many of my 101 classes were similar in size to high school. Others were huge with a couple hundred students.

Once acclimated, I embraced college as my new home and way of life. I created a daily schedule to balance my academic and social objectives. I finished my classes, hung out on campus, completed my homework by 6:00 p.m. and partied.

My passion for soccer never subsided. I played on an intramural soccer team called The Squirrel Nuts. Half the team comprised of players I played with in high school. With a great deal of talent for an intramural team we won the majority of season championships.

Each Thursday night one of the fraternities held a party. I attended because a friend in the fraternity wanted me to rush. I didn't want to rush but wanted exclusive access to big private parties. In typical fashion I showed off, told half-truth stories, and drew attention to myself.

On a particular Thursday, my frat friend purchased a huge tub of hot cocoa from Costco. In a drunken stupor, I kicked the tub of hot cocoa. It burst open onto the bedroom floor. He chased me out of the room with swords coming out of his mouth.

I hid from him and snuck back into the room. I convinced a different friend to grab handfuls of the hot cocoa and dump it into a fan. Set on high speed, the entire room became a cloud of cocoa powder. I destroyed my friend's room but people laughed. I accomplished my goal to be known.

College parties offered many opportunities to hook up with girls. Nobody knew my virgin secret because of the stories I told in high school. I viewed my virgin status as a failure. I bought into the cultural lie that virgins aren't cool. The college atmosphere wasn't conducive for my high school lies.

I needed to remedy the situation before being outed as a fraud. In fall of my freshman year I met an attractive girl. She lived in the dorms. We liked each other and hung out often. We partied together and shared similar interests. After a month or two we slept together at a party.

I expected to feel vindicated and a member of the gentleman's club. I expected to feel transformed and hear birds sing melodies for me. I bragged about my accomplishment. I even teased other virgins to make them feel inferior.

In reality, I experienced the opposite effect. She genuinely liked me and wanted a relationship. I genuinely liked her too. But the possibility of a pregnancy terrified me. I ignored her. I disregarded her feelings and pushed her away.

Blinded by my selfish ambitions, I treated her like an object of accomplishment. I didn't understand the impacts and ripple effect of my decision. Our tension and strife separated mutual friendships. Our genuine friendship ended in a broken relationship.

I remained in the dorms throughout my freshman year. Being surrounded by thousands of likeminded college kids still didn't eradicate my sorrow. The lack of curfew and house rules didn't heal my heart. I relied on music, alcohol, jewelry, long hair, and cologne for treatment. In reality, how I used them poisoned me. But I couldn't stop.

Several of my high school friends who didn't attended college visited often. I didn't want my relationship with them to diminish. But the distance and time apart strained our relationship. Over time, we saw each other less and less. I struggled with the change because of my loyalty to them. I didn't want my friends to feel abandoned. I blamed myself for leaving them in the Tri-Cities.

My body posture revealed the effects of years of downcast thoughts. One day the RA in our dorm said, "Bill, I know you are sad. Every time I see you, you are looking down at the ground."

Suicidal thoughts often consumed my mind. I dreamt of different ways to end my life. The more I focused on my worthlessness, the more I didn't care. Tougher days yielded worse results.

The night before winter quarter began brought my pain to a head. I watched *Beverly Hills 90210* and *Melrose Place* with two of my female friends. By the time the two shows ended, I had finished a bottle of rum. I stumbled back to my dorm room. I dropped the empty bottle of rum on the floor and it shattered. I then blacked out.

I woke up the next morning on a couch in our dorm floor commons area. A garbage can lay next to me on the ground. My friend slept on the couch adjacent to me. "I was very worried about you," he said, "and almost called the ambulance. I thought you were going to die."

So many things contributed to me not liking me. Eastern hosted a melting pot of different races. I didn't feel like the minority anymore. But my friends and I developed a bad habit of demeaning other races. Many times I weathered the brunt of those jokes. We used every slang and derogatory word known at the time. People even addressed me by a derogatory word instead of my first name.

Some comments were brutal and blatant. I heard, "Shut up Bill, you're just a flip," or "You brown piece of crap, you swam over the ocean on a banana leaf."

I laughed and played along. I pretended the words deflected off me. But I never realized how deep the words cut. They wore me down and wounded me. Over time I associated my brown skin as a defect.

At a party with my friends, the verbal barrage continued. I broke down in front of them. "I can't take being called these names anymore, it hurts so much."

"We had no idea they *really* bothered you because you always just laughed and played along."

My identity seemed lost. I continued searching for significance. I welcomed opportunities to fit in. Hip-hop and grunge music influenced my curiosity to smoke weed. I tried weed a couple times in high school. The effects didn't interest me. However, the persona of weed attracted me. I preferred joints. I created giant billows of smoke around my head. The billows made me feel tough and cool.

I purchased a joint roller around spring time. I quickly became proficient at rolling doobies. An anonymous donor sent me a softball sized clump of marijuana to my dorm room mailbox. I am uncertain how a standard envelope with a giant bulge in the middle made it through the post office. Nevertheless, I rolled joints in my dorm room for hours. I handed them out for free to whoever wanted one. I refused to sell joints because I didn't want the drug dealer label.

I continued to associate alcohol use with popularity. My professor in my Chicano class required all students to give a speech. I accepted a dare to slam shots before my class. The alcohol gave me the liquid courage to orate to the almost one-hundred students. I reveled in the lore that created for months.

I even split a bottle of vodka with three teammates before an intramural playoff soccer game. I made a fool of myself on the field. We lost and the rest of the team reproached me. The director of intramural sports almost expelled me from all sports programs. Common sense didn't click in my tumultuous mind.

I approached the final quarter of my freshman year. One Friday, I caught a glimpse of an attractive girl as she stepped into the dorm room elevator. At first glance I thought, *She is way out of my league.* Nevertheless, I asked around to see if anyone knew her. I don't know where the courage to do so came from.

I found out her name and what dorm she lived in. We eventually met through a mutual friend. After a few weeks of introductions, we dated. I still carried the way-out-of-my-league complex. Many guys commented, "How did you get a girl like her?"

Our relationship grew and we became more intimate. I spent more and more time with her. I met her wonderful family. But my insecurities and lack of confidence plagued me. I compared myself to her beauty, social status, and academic acumen.

I compared myself to her previous boyfriends. I lacked many of their qualities. I worried about what her parents wanted for their daughter. I believed other people's accusations of inadequacy, including my own.

I strained to live up to false expectations I thought she required of me. I cut back on my alcohol intake. I tried to astonish her with my vast collection of hip-hop and R&B albums. I wanted to be the sexy and romantic man in the bedroom. I strived to please her.

I committed my time and resources to make her happy. I desperately wanted her to love me.

CHAPTER NINE

I Found Me, I Think

I FINISHED MY first year at EWU. I cherished the memories and new friendships I created. My freshman year solidified my purpose in life: college. College life became my reason for existence.

I moved back to Richland for summer break. Compared to my life at EWU, I considered Richland beneath me. I worked full time on a farm throughout summer. Up at 5:00 a.m. and home at 6:00 p.m. five days a week. An additional half day on Saturdays left little time for extracurricular activities.

I made several trips to Spokane to visit my girlfriend. Each time I did I longed to get back to my college life. September approached. My parents gave me their 1986 faded-yellow Oldsmobile Cutlass Supreme. My roommate from my freshman year moved into a townhouse with another friend. I moved in with two other friends into a cheap apartment my sophomore year. Very cheap.

With effort, a person could see through the crack in the front door. The carpet resembled something from an abandoned house. The sliding glass door in the living room didn't completely shut. Small snow drifts collected in the corner of our living room in the winter.

With a year under my belt I navigated easily around campus. I recognized more and more people. I did well in my 201 classes. I lounged in my comfort zone of freedom. My childish antics flared up often in class. I distracted students, instigated laughter, and annoyed professors.

I dated my girlfriend through my sophomore year in college. I spent more time with my girlfriend and less time with my friends. I split time between them and her when I partied. I hung out with my friends for a few hours. I drank as much as possible as fast as possible.

Then I vanished without notice. They resented her and held a grudge against me. The police pulled me over a few times on the way to her apartment. Only by God's grace did I not ever receive a DUI.

I battled my ongoing struggle of not being good enough. The slightest bit of attraction she felt for other men made me paranoid. I wanted her to be attracted to me alone.

I loved my girlfriend and wanted to be with her. In December I asked her to marry me. But, inside, I feared marriage. I liked the idea of marriage but remained naïve to the commitment. She focused on the future. I lived in the past. She desired children. I dreaded children. She prepared for a nice career. I pursued the next college party.

I coveted a storybook relationship. I wanted to be the perfect husband, the perfect son-in-law. My fiancée was an amazing woman. Her parents treated me like royalty, like a son. But I couldn't bear the pressure from my own insecurities. I realized the mirage of marriage in my mind couldn't fix my brokenness. After a couple months of engagement I made the decision to call off the wedding.

An unexpected death in the family changed my plans and introduced a new level of chaos in my mind. I thought, "There's no way I can break up with her now. That would be too devastating."

I cast aside my own well-being and buried my internal raging war. I turned my attention away from me to support her family.

I pledged to make a lifelong commitment of support for her sake. I vowed to cover up my agony to proceed with the marriage. I tried to make our relationship work. I stayed in the relationship into my junior year.

I still struggled with my identity and hung onto the gangsta image. I purchased a handgun. The power of the gun at the shooting range hypnotized me. When I pulled the trigger, the shockwave and concussion fascinated me. The gun helped me vent frustration and anger. But the false sense of strength and power gave me a false sense of security and value.

By March my interest in the gangsta image and attire lessened. I switched to normal jeans, tennis shoes and inside out sweaters. I wore my Raiders hat but only to keep my long hair out of my face.

Despite the change in attire I continued to experience different forms of racism. One weekend I went with a group of people to Vancouver, Canada. One of my friends invited some guys that looked like poster children for marijuana.

Four stoned Caucasians and I arrived at the border in one car. The U.S. Customs and Border Protection asked questions. A couple of us said different things. An officer singled me out. He instructed us to pull forward so I could be searched. I exited the vehicle.

The officer didn't pay one iota of attention to my hippie friends. Instead, he dropped my suitcase on the ground and rummaged through it. The officer's body language and facial expressions communicated prejudice. When he finished he said, "You can go through now." He left my suitcase open on the ground. Some of my stuff lay on the pavement. He cracked a few of my CD cases in the process. I stood in the open, humiliated, while my friends and strangers watched the entire incident.

My fragile state of mind persisted through my sophomore year. Our apartment manager installed a portable basketball hoop near our apartment. My roommates and I often played horse or one on one. While we played one day, the apartment manager said, "Dude, you are so small. Can you even get the ball all the way up to the basket?" He then bellowed a loud and shallow laugh.

His rude and arrogant comments continued throughout my length of stay in our apartment. Like many other hurtful comments, I played them off as trivial. But, over time, the accumulation of those comments pierced me.

Deflated, I plunged further into hopelessness. I experimented with different genres of music to help me cope. I needed more mental isolation. For several months I listened to ENYA and Nirvana almost every day. I heard the song "Dumb" from Nirvana's MTV *Unplugged in New York* album. The lyrics spoke to me. I repeated the song while I walked around campus. I uttered the lyrics under my breath over and over.

I believed those words. I discovered the *psychology department* at Eastern offered cash awards to participate in various studies. I volunteered for a study on depression. The students sat me down in a room. I listened to a variety of classical songs. Afterwards, they asked me a series of questions to describe my feelings.

I told them not one particular song made me feel happy. But I pointed out which ones made me sad. They looked at each other and then me. One asked, "Are you sure you feel that way? Those songs were supposed to make you feel happy."

My sophomore year came to an end. I procrastinated to the last second and scrambled to select a major. I didn't care about my major because I didn't attend college for an education. I stood in line the last day of registration. I scanned through the catalog of bachelor degree options. I shook my head at all the major options like history, math and biology. I thought, *I am not smart enough to do any of these.*

I panicked as I approached the registration tables. Then I saw communications: public speaking and interpersonal communications. "That sounds easy. I don't need to be smart to take those classes. Now my studying won't interrupt the next two years of partying." A lame way to choose a degree.

I didn't move back to the Tri-Cities in summer. I outgrew my roots. I attended summer school and lived with my aunt and uncle in Spokane. They loved me and nurtured my relationship with Jesus. I looked to them as my Christian mentors. They encouraged me and being around them made me feel like a better person. I drank only a few times my sophomore summer.

I landed a job at the campus athletic center in June. The athletic center included a dance studio, a weight room, and facilities for the popular sports. The skills required for the job came naturally to me. I set up the sports courts and equipment by 6:00 a.m. each morning. I checked out sports gear to different classes and students.

I liked the atmosphere of the facility. It exuded energy and activity. I managed the weight room during my shift. Day after day I watched athletic men and women work out. I despised my scrawny skin-and-bones physique. Sick and tired of being called twerp and runt, I started lifting weights.

I determined to be strong and gain weight. I related to the movie *Rudy* when the character Fortune said, "You are five foot nothin', a hundred and nothin', and hardly have a spec of athletic ability."

I lifted weights five days a week from June through September. When my junior year started I weighed 175 pounds with about nine to ten percent body fat. Not quite the Incredible Hulk, but I gained forty pounds of solid muscle. My athletic ability increased and I ran a forty-yard dash just under 4.3 seconds. With my vertical jump, I grabbed the basketball rim with ease.

Friends who returned from summer break couldn't believe their eyes. My confidence skyrocketed and girls noticed me more. My social bubble increased. I hung out with players on the women's volleyball team and the men's football team. My notoriety and popularity soared. I played intramural soccer, volleyball, and basketball. I received the attention I wanted for years. My fiancé liked my new body. She didn't like the extra looks from other females.

I lifted weights the remainder of time in college. The health and sports benefits I received from strength training were bonuses. But I primarily lifted so others would notice me. I despised being one of the smallest guys on campus. Muscle mass gave me identity and value. I added weight lifting to my repertoire of escape options.

I scheduled daily activities around my lifting routine. If I skipped a few days, I panicked. I worried I would shrink back down to my old size. I believed without my new body I would return to nothing once again. Time invested in the gym helped me deal with my anguish. Recounted mistakes provided the motivation for each leg press or bench press.

Before my physical transformation, when I played soccer I did it with a nothing-to-lose mentality. I didn't play dirty but I intended to win every ball. My new strength and size elevated my average level of physical play to an extraordinary level. I released pent up anger and frustration into every header, slide tackle and 50/50 ball. Risk of injury didn't concern me. My opponents suffered the wrath of my tumult.

But my new body and benefits didn't deliver me from my heartache. My good friend said to me, "You know, a lot of bodybuilders and guys who spend so much time lifting weights are unhappy and are trying to fix something."

I dismissed his arrogant comment. But the truth of his words pierced me. My extra strength couldn't sustain the mounting pressure of my engagement. I second-guessed my decision to stay in the relationship for my fiancé's sake. But I didn't give up yet.

My new physique, increased confidence, and social status propelled me through fall quarter of my junior year. The communications classes were much smaller and more focused. I uncovered a hidden natural gift for speaking and communicating. I studied hard and refined my public speaking skills.

A few of us established a reputation within the department as the best communicators. I developed a passion for writing speeches. Different communication styles and techniques intrigued me. My favorite professor taught a course on persuasion. He assigned the class to write and present a ten-minute speech for our final.

Ten minutes seemed like an eternity. But I prepared for hours. I crafted the flow and chose the right descriptive language, similes, and metaphors. I memorized most of the speech. I watched several students present their speeches. Some did well, some nearly passed out from stress and nervousness.

I compared what I wrote to the other students' speeches. Doubt grew each time someone presented. I went last. Comfortable and composed, I gave my speech. The words flowed from my mouth. I finished with poise. The class congratulated me with a loud applause.

I looked up at the clock and asked my professor, "Oops, it wasn't quite ten minutes. I hope that's okay?"

He looked at me while tears welled up in his eyes. "It was perfect." My professor wrote on the front page of my final paper "Epideictic in its highest form!"

I didn't have a clue what epideictic meant. A few days later he said, "Bill, that was the greatest speech I have ever heard from any of my students."

Fall quarter ended on a high note. The crescendo of college life intensified. I lived in a dream.

But, a few weeks into January, I called off my engagement. I surrendered. I collapsed under the mental, physical, and emotional stress. My fiancé didn't deserve a lifelong lie. My decision devastated her. The news rippled throughout her circle of friends. Her friends ostracized me. My friends consoled me.

Her family suffered the pain of my decision too. About a month later her mom called me on the phone. "I have to know, did you want to end the relationship before or after the tragedy in my family?" I paused. I could protect the family or tell the truth. I chose to protect the family. "After."

Disappointment resonated in her mom's voice. "How could you?" She said I became like a son to them. And the break-up felt like another death in the family.

A lance of guilt impaled my heart. I punished myself. For twenty years I repeated those words over and over in my mind. I leaned into alcohol, music, and weights to reinforce my prison walls. The cells and corridors became more numerous.

In spring quarter I reverted to poetry to express my feelings. In my sociology class I came across the poem "Suicide Note" by Janice Mirikitani. The book *Race, Class, and Gender in the United States* contained the poem. I believed it summarized my entire existence. I gulped when I read the lines from the poem.

For several months I obsessed over the poem. I read it before I slept at night. I daydreamed about it in class. Each time it affected my heart rate and breathing. I wanted to proclaim to the world what I found. I wanted to hand people the poem and say, "If you want to know me, read this "Suicide Note." This is who I am."

CHAPTER TEN

No Hope and No Healing

I LIVED IN a duplex with my female cousin my junior and senior years. We turned our home into a social hub. Her friends and my friends interacted well together. We hosted many parties and sleepovers. Our living situation worked in my favor.

I flirted with many of her friends. But I sought attention from women in general. In most cases, I deemed a female's social status, appearance, and reputation irrelevant. If a girl noticed me, I noticed her.

I craved regular interactions with females. Many encounters were non-sexual in nature. On several occasions different girls slept in my room. Many nights my cousin's friends slept in my bed. On other nights girls I knew from college slept in my bed. Sexual attraction existed, but I craved companionship.

Little doses of affection coursed through my veins when females gave me attention. Quick pecks on the lips with a girl at a party or in a bar electrified my soul. I fed on the nutrients of hope those moments provided. But a bad encounter with a female wiped out ten good encounters. Rejection obliterated my confidence and self-worth.

While in the full swing of my upperclassman years I turned twenty-one before most of my friends. I celebrated at Showies, the local college pub, with an older friend. Upon my entrance a couple people shouted, "You finally made it."

After a few beers, I realized the bar scene offered a realm of new possibilities. I went to my 11:00 a.m. communications class the next day hung over. But my previous night's experience birthed a new world of social independence.

I began a routine of bar hopping. Towards summer, my friends and I found Outback Jacks in downtown Spokane. The club held a college night every Thursday. We planned our entire week around Thursday. I cashed my paychecks to spend at the club.

Our mission, never miss a night. On the rare occasion we did, I stressed out and panicked. I felt robbed of missed opportunities and memories.

We often arrived around 6:00 p.m. to secure a table next to the dance floor. We drank and danced until 1:00 a.m. – 1:30 am. I came home, slept a few hours and woke up at 5:00 a.m. to work my 6:00 a.m. athletic center shift. The atmosphere and energy of club life superceded the need for sleep.

Over time my identity crisis worsened. I grasped onto movie characters, athletes, and superheroes. The movie *Tombstone* captivated me. The character Doc Holliday played by Val Kilmer fascinated me. I mimicked his accent and his mannerisms. I memorized his quotes. I dropped lines from the movie at parties or in the middle of conversations. I dressed up as Doc Holliday for a Halloween party.

The movie *Leaving Las Vegas* left a similar imprint on my mind. I admired the character Ben Sanderson played by Nicolas Cage. I imitated his actions and one-liners too. I glorified his intoxicated behavior. I wanted to emulate his drinking binges.

I practically worshiped Michael Jordan, Scotty Pippen, and Dennis Rodman, especially Rodman. I idolized him more than any other human being for years. I saw parts of me in Rodman. His persona and uniqueness attracted me. I believed he was the greatest defender and rebounder in NBA history. I lived vicariously through his success on the basketball court. I compared Dennis's career to what my career could have been through soccer.

I even idolized cartoon characters. I fancied the character Gambit from the 90s *X-Men* cartoon. I acted like him and tried to imitate his Cajun accent. I chased after people and fictitious characters for significance and identity. I glorified and exalted the fantasy of their personas.

The allure of the military also offered another identity option. Several of my friends graduated high school and joined the military. Their boot camp stories and various tours fascinated me. I interrogated them with questions about a day in the life of military personnel.

My interested surged when I watched the Army ROTC students. They drilled and trained in the early mornings at the athletic center. I imagined what my life would be like in the military. I inquired about my grandpa's service in the navy in WW II at Iwo Jima. I started to equate all military personnel as heroes. I wanted to be a hero.

I looked to an array of external sources to give me value and purpose. My cousin purchased a new computer. I used the computer primarily to play video games. I bought the game Warcraft. I installed the game and watched the intro cinematic scene. I was hooked.

I immersed myself into the RPG world. I had never experienced such deep storylines and well developed characters before. The expansive environments, engaging music, and sound effects captivated me. Addicted, I played for hours at a time.

I wanted to play whenever an opportunity presented itself. I headed to WSU on a Saturday to visit a friend and party at his apartment. I escaped into his bedroom to play a couple computer games. I played for four hours. During those four hours several people arrived at his apartment. People were dumbfounded when I came out of the bedroom. "Whoa, where did you come from and who are you? Were you in there the whole time?"

Video games distracted me from my pain. They camouflaged my denial. My mind and emotions teleported into games. The shell of my physical body remained in the chair. I convinced myself *I can't get hurt inside here. I can't disappoint anyone in here. I can't make mistakes in here.*

The make believe world blurred the lines between the real world. The make believe world pleased my senses and emotions. I developed a false sense of reality as a result.

I discovered another make believe world on the PC, AOL. At the time, AOL dominated the ISP world. A five-minute wait to get connected online didn't bother me. I looked forward to the "Welcome" and "You've Got Mail" greetings.

The Internet unlocked an unexplored world of fantasy. The chat rooms fascinated me the most. The simultaneous interaction with multiple people all over the country intrigued me. In my element, I jumped into conversations with no hesitation. I embellished stories, bragged about college life and shared music interests.

I created "Tears21" as my first AOL chatroom name. People asked why I chose my screenname. I explained to them my sadness. I shared lines from my poems laced with sorrow and emptiness. Responses like, "You brought me to tears" coddled me. I wrote lines about a fictitious woman I loved. I treasured comments from women who said, "I want to be that woman."

Despite my internal struggle I continued to excel in my communications classes. Public speaking assignments and projects came more easily my senior year. I excelled in my social life too. I remained active and played intramural soccer, volleyball, and pick-up basketball. My employment continued at the athletic center.

I rubbed shoulders with players from the women's volleyball team, the women's dance team, and the men's football team. My physique stayed solid. Full of confidence, I often removed my shirt at parties. I danced with girls and soaked up the attention.

I knew many people and my social status flourished. I often sat on the sitting wall that stretched across the front of the Pence Union Building (PUB), the epicenter of campus where students interacted between classes and for lunch. I watched the busyness of campus life as people passed by. I high fived guys, hugged girls, laughed, and carried on.

My friends and I gathered inside the PUB several times a week. We played blackjack for quarters, spoons, and other card games. We drew attention with our loud conversations and exuberant antics. I became addicted to the routine of people watching and playing games. Those experiences produced a high better than chemicals or alcohol.

I traveled to Richland for Christmas break. I stayed at my parents' house. I celebrated New Year's Eve at a bar with friends, the last New Year's Eve as a college student. I expected to experience a night full of fanfare and fun. But the night started and ended like a deflated balloon. A few moments after midnight I left for my parents' house.

My life revolved around parties, clubs, dancing, and women. I cared about one day at a time and one party at a time. My denial of the future exponentially increased. Bitterness crept in when winter quarter ended. I realized graduation loomed around the corner. I refused to face the truth of college only lasting four years. I refused to accept that my whole way of life would soon shatter.

I returned to school and started spring quarter. More and more of my thoughts were consumed with the end of college. Many nights I laid in bed with headphones. I listened to songs from artists like Chris Isaak, ENYA and Az Yet.

I closed my eyes in pain. The lyrics and melody of the songs painted visions and landscapes of my desperate desire to be loved. I imagined a train conductor saying, "All aboard. It's time to take a grand tour of the corridors of your mind."

Then the conductor announced, "Next stop, worthlessness. We'll spend some time here then move on to the next stop, anger." The tour continued for about an hour. I soaked my headphones and pillow with tears. I sighed and fell asleep.

My toughest moment in life came on graduation day in March 1997. The magnitude of the day crushed me. Graduation wasn't supposed to come. I wasn't supposed to wake from my dream. I counted on denial to shield me from ever facing the truth. I stood at the exit door of college with no future and no plans.

During the ceremony my gut wrenched and my palms were sweaty. None of my friends graduated with me. I went to summer school and they didn't. I only recognized a few people. The ceremony, unlike high school, was very somber for me.

The announcer called my name. I walked up slowly to get my degree. No newspaper photographer took my picture. I didn't stand up and scream or shout. I didn't celebrate my GPA of just under 3.5. I received my degree with a halfhearted smile. I strolled out of the gym with tears in my eyes.

I invested my college years trying to fill the void inside my heart. I built a perfect life. I attended a four-year university. I sculpted my body to a peak of physical fitness. I elevated my social status. I rose in popularity and women liked me. I surrounded myself with lots of friends. I partied all the time. I lived the dream of a college kid.

Those things never healed me. They never gave me hope. They never truly satisfied me. I relied on external things to fill my void. But my heart remained a floodplain of tears and a swamp of sorrows. At the end of college, the needle in the tank of my heart pointed to empty.

CHAPTER ELEVEN

Bound by Chains

FOR SEVERAL DAYS after graduation I sulked. "Now what do I do?" The real world crashed into me. My fantasy bubble popped violently. I knew nothing except college life. Graduation forced me to leave the comfort and safety of college.

My aunt and uncle in Spokane offered their home to me. I lived in their downstairs bedroom. They continued to mentor me in the Bible and taught me about Jesus. My desire to know more about Jesus increased. Little by little God opened my eyes to His love.

My knowledge of God increased. The certainty of responsibility did too. I shifted into a "fly-by-the-seat-of-my-pants" mode. I needed to find a job. But I made zero effort at Eastern to prepare myself for a career. Clueless and without any business acumen, I freaked out. My resume looked like crap. I wasn't motivated to hunt for jobs. I didn't know what I wanted to do or how to find out.

I interviewed with a couple national companies and a few local companies. They turned me down after the first round. Pressure mounted after several failed attempts. I didn't want to fail my parents. They paid for most of my college tuition and expenses. I couldn't let them down.

After about a month of job hunting, I attended a career fair. I met the branch manager for a major insurance company. We clicked and he interviewed me a few days later. After several conversations he seemed impressed. "I want to hire you but I can't until you pass the state required insurance exam." Certain I would pass the test he began the preliminary steps to hire me.

I doubted my qualifications from the day we met. Despite the branch manager's eagerness to hire me, I thought, *I am not good enough; I am not smart enough; I don't have what it takes.* Extensive and intense, the insurance exam lasted over an hour. I didn't know the answer to most of the initial questions. *I knew I had already failed and I gave up.* I filled in boxes and made up answers to complete the test. I left the interview dejected.

I met the branch manager a few days later. He shook my hand with a puzzled look on his face. "I really wanted to hire you but you didn't pass the test. I would love to try again if you go out and get some experience."

I subjected myself to too many rejections. I stopped applying at big companies. I settled for the want ads. I responded to an outside sales job for a small alarm company. I talked to the owner over the phone and then met for a face-to-face interview. He hired me on the spot.

The company employed less than ten people. I didn't mind. I landed my first real world job. A salary of $1,000 a month blew me away. I struck gold compared to my $4.44 an hour wage at the EWU athletic center. I called many of my college friends to brag.

I started my career green and inexperienced. But each day I gained more tenure and my confidence increased. I became friends with my boss and we hung out a few times. He showed me the ropes of the alarm system trade.

After a few months at my aunt and uncle's house, I moved out. I rented an apartment in Spokane with a close friend from college. A perfect fit for both of us. Neither of us were ready to give up our dream life. I paid rent for him for a couple months while he searched for a job.

I backslid into my college comfort zone. I remained trapped in denial. I tried to recreate remnants of the past. My roommate and I survived off the crumbs of college memories. I hung out on campus, crashed parties, and went to Showies. I partied at Outback Jack's each Thursday night.

I frequently escaped into the world of computer game fantasy. I played endless hours of Diablo and Starcraft. I daydreamed about different weapons, armor upgrades, and special items. I dropped one-liners from the games in everyday conversations. I counted on my video games for solace after a stressful day.

But each day passed and the luster of my previous life faded. My vice grip on college slowly loosened. My social status disappeared into the sea of Spokanites. My already brittle identity weakened. Most people were strangers. The real world ripped away my sense of belonging.

I gradually learned how to be a responsible adult but I struggled to adapt to the real world. It contained no semblance of the protected bubble of my college life. Reality seemed much bigger and less friendly.

I joined a gym and a men's city soccer league. I didn't want my physique and athleticism to atrophy. I still needed my strength to shoulder the burdens in my life. The thought of not having my physical gifts terrified me. I feared the worst case scenario: losing an extremity, a limb, or becoming physically disabled. Without my body whole and healthy I could not survive.

I ran the feeble body scenario through my mind a 1,000 times. I concluded suicide would be the only option. I planned to buy a cyanide pill to keep on me at all times as an easy escape if I ever became incapacitated for any reason.

I told some close friends about my idea. I expected agreement and understanding. Instead, they reprimanded me. "Why would you need that? You said you trusted God. If you truly believe that then you can't have a cyanide pill. You need to trust Him." I didn't buy a cyanide pill.

I needed other solutions to deal with my distress. I got my first tattoo in the summer, something I wanted since I turned eighteen. But I wanted to wait until I graduated college. If I still wanted a tattoo after four years, then I knew I wouldn't regret it.

I went to Tiger Tattoo in Spokane. I provided the tattoo artist a description of what I wanted: Jesus on the cross with vines surrounding Him. Black ink and on my lower back. She drew a perfect template.

Tattoos weren't as popular among the youth at that time. I didn't get my tattoo as a social statement or to be rebellious. I required it to deal with my pain. When I gazed at my tattoo in the mirror I responded in two different ways: "Look what you have done for me, Jesus" and "Look what I have done to you, Jesus."

I loved showing off my tattoo. I didn't need an excuse to remove my shirt. I showed people at the basketball court, soccer field, and at the clubs. People's reactions of intrigue and interest encouraged me.

I wanted my Tri-Cities friends to see it too. I called a close friend in Richland to tell him. Our conversation sparked interest in a camping trip. We met over a long weekend at Wallowa Lake, Oregon. The campground and scenery reminded me of my childhood camping trips. The smell of the pine trees, the sound of a fresh water stream, and the majestic mountains took my breath away.

We fished, played card games, and explored the campground. We burned a large fire at night. We reminisced and shared our lives with each other. The camping trip revitalized me.

I went home refreshed and relaxed. The trip provided a reprieve from the pressures of life. My friends and I planned another trip the following year.

I returned to work ready to succeed. I gave my parents back their Oldsmobile Cutlass Supreme. My dad bought me a 1990, blood-orange Chevy S-10 pickup. I spent hours in my truck for my sales job. I drove to homes and businesses throughout Spokane County. Most days I listened to KZZU-FM (The Zoo) on my commute. During my commute one day in August, I hit the scan button on my radio. The frequency landed on Praise 106.5 and God interrupted my life.

I tuned into the middle of a sermon by Pastor John Hagee. Sermons were unfamiliar to me. I only attended the traditional Christmas Eve and Easter church services as a kid. His boisterous and commanding voice grabbed my attention. The authority with which he spoke on the Bible and Jesus amazed me.

I heard truths about Jesus and what He thought of me for the first time. I hungered for more. I regularly tuned into sermons on the radio. I discovered more pastors and ministries. I listened to Dr. David Jeremiah, Pastor Chuck Swindoll, Pastor Greg Laurie, and Dr. James Dobson.

Then I learned about TBN from the radio. I watched sermons on the radio and TV. My commute became my favorite part of the day. Day after day I grew in my faith. My walk with Jesus blossomed.

At the same time the words in the sermons were contrary to my thoughts. My mind was unaccustomed to life-giving words. Mistakes, guilt, and shame were familiar to me. I understood worthlessness, fear, and rejection. But I learned about forgiveness, grace, and mercy. I learned about unconditional love, purpose, and identity.

Radio and television ministry became my church. I didn't know much, but my heart exploded with joy. I wanted others to know what I learned. I shared Jesus with people in my circle of influence. I shared Him with my friends, people at parties and with my co-workers.

My conversations with my aunt and uncle changed. I often called my uncle to ask him about something I heard in a sermon.

I understood more about what they taught me. My aunt and uncle rejoiced over my newly-found hope.

I also quickly learned not everyone shared the same excitement as me. Some people listened, others dismissed me. Others were indifferent and shrugged their shoulders. I am confident my theology wasn't always accurate.

My life started changing. But my old self warred against the truth of the Bible. I couldn't break free from the chains in my mind. I didn't escape the prison of my mind.

CHAPTER TWELVE

Good-bye Glory Days

I BECAME MORE proficient four months into my career. My skills improved as an outside sales professional. In early September my boss informed me the Spokane branch would close. He wanted to move his business to western Washington. He asked if I would relocate too.

I wrestled with the decision for two weeks. Conflict and mixed emotions flooded my mind. I didn't want to ruin the perfect setup with my friend and roommate. I didn't want to abandon my college life. How could I leave behind the life I created in eastern Washington?

But I didn't want to job hunt again. I wanted to escape the shame I created with my ex-fiancé and her family. I needed to run from my past. I resolved to relinquish the grip on my old fantasy life.

In October 1997, I made the excruciating decision to move. I knew the moment I left Spokane things would never be the same again. I loathed moving day. I hugged my friend and roommate. I barely mustered the strength to say good-bye. I left a huge piece of my heart in Cheney and Spokane.

In the process of making the decision to move, I also made a gut-wrenching oath. I would cease efforts to make new friends. I invested years into a handful of deep relationships from high school and college. I believed with certainty I would never form similar friendships again. I decreed no person post-college deserved the right to have a relationship with me. Nobody could earn it.

I turned my friendship switch off. I intentionally avoided new friendships. My deep-rooted fear of abandonment protected me. I erected a barricade. I went into survivor mode. Independent and self-sustained, I determined to do life alone. I didn't need anyone. I validated my emotions based on a scene from the movie *Tuskegee Airmen*. My best defense against losing a friend was to not make any more.

I departed Spokane in a U-Haul. Gloom and grief came with me. I moved into an apartment in Auburn, Washington, with my boss. I didn't know anyone else. I lived in misery for three months. Fleas infested the apartment. I didn't know the city and my bank account suffered.

Dark and dreary weather became the norm. Ninety days of rain fell in a 120-day period. The rubber seal around my windshield failed. Almost every morning I drove to work with my feet in about an inch of water.

For three months I regretted the move to western Washington. I struggled to adjust to my new environment and life. I relied on a *Thomas Guide* for directions to my sales appointments. Inexperienced at reading maps I lost my way many times. I wandered for hours trying to locate addresses. I closed few sales and missed many appointments. Lost in a strange land with no friends, I yearned to go back to Spokane.

Around December my roommate from Spokane moved to Seattle. His friendship provided comfort for me. We hung out almost every weekend. In late winter of 1999 we moved into an apartment together. We lived in the U District by the University of Washington. We enabled each other's stubborn grasp on the past.

We relived fragments of memories. We inserted ourselves into the U of W college atmosphere.

I drank many nights. I frequented Dante's, the local university pub, and flirted with women. I still craved attention from women. I watched for women who noticed me. A woman who flirted with me injected confidence into my veins, a momentary relief from my loneliness.

My boss's ex-girlfriend from Spokane also moved to the Seattle area. She worked at the Spokane branch for a while. We knew each other on a platonic level. We decided to hang out with a group of friends at Dante's. The plan—relax and have fun, nothing more.

After several drinks we flirted with each other. I could not resist the opportunity. Around midnight we went to my place. We slept together and she stayed the night.

I didn't wake up and celebrate. I didn't brag. Guilt and shame dominated my thoughts. Her being my boss's ex-girlfriend made me feel awkward and uncomfortable. We didn't see each other again.

I'd slept with three women in my life at that point. My relationship void increased. To compensate, I turned to sexual stimulation and pleasure. I took advantage of slow appointment days. When I was alone in my apartment, I'd walk to a Blockbuster down the street and rent B movies filled with nudity and sexual scenes. I skipped to the sex scenes.

I repeated the habit many times. Embarrassed and full of shame, I returned the movies to the Blockbuster counter. One time, an employee said, "Wow, you rent a lot of movies from us." I perceived his thoughts as he looked at the movie titles. His facial expression made them obvious. My addiction to sexual stimulation didn't satisfy my heart's longing for real relationship.

But, in the midst of my tempest, Jesus comforted me. He gave me hope. My friends and I went to Wallowa Lake on Memorial Day weekend of 1998. The campground hovered around ninety degrees.

We rode the gondola up to the mountain lodge. Snow covered the ground a couple feet deep.

We explored the mountain around the lodge. We sledded on our bellies down small slopes. We threw snowballs at each other. I wandered off by myself. I walked to the edge of the mountain. The view overlooked the ridges between two other mountains. A thin layer of fog filled the air. The sun stood above the ridge between the two mountains.

Jesus called to me. I looked up. I gazed directly into the sun. It didn't hurt my eyes. I didn't squint. *Look at my wonders*, He said. A deluge of peace and love washed over me. His love overwhelmed me. I returned from my camping trip refreshed and revitalized.

I pressed into my career. I became fluent in my trade and confident in my sales appointments. I increased my sales numbers month over month. My boss promoted me to sales manager in summer.

I continued to work hard. In fall 1998, our company hosted an awards ceremony dinner. They awarded me "Employee of the Year." I received an engraved plaque—my first employee recognition in a real world job. My parents were proud and my friends congratulated me.

The award presented an interesting dichotomy. In one aspect it symbolized accomplishment and hard work. In another aspect it exposed my wound of I am not good enough. I believed, *I don't deserve an award. I don't deserve honor or recognition. I am a horrible person.*

But I hung onto the notion of success the award represented. After all, I uprooted my life and moved to an unfamiliar city. I persevered through tough times in my young career. My award offered a small reprieve from my mountains of mistakes. It offered a glimmer of redemption from my ugliness.

But a single phrase robbed me of the delight of my award. An acquaintance said at a party, "Your award doesn't count. Your company is so small. It doesn't mean anything."

I believed him. Who was I trying to fool? I took the award home and tucked it away.

By May I navigated Puget Sound with ease. My commute in Puget Sound required much more driving than in Spokane. I drove approximately 250 miles a day. I continued to listen to the radio. I divided my radio time into two opposing parts.

Half the time I listened to the most popular radio station in western Washington. They played hip hop and claimed the number one morning show spot. The other half of my time I listened to sermons on Praise 106.5. One moment I pumped my ears full of discussions about sex, alcohol, and parties. In another moment I absorbed and ingested the life-giving words of the Bible.

I noticed Puget Sound contained just about every variety of vehicle made. I grew tired of my boring truck. I learned of other Chevy S-10 owners who did V-8 conversions. I set my mind on doing my own.

I surmised several hundred horsepower would vanquish my frustration and anger. The sense of power and speed would substitute for my lack and insecurities. I convinced my parents to loan me $5,000 to do the V-8 conversion.

My boss referred me to a guy in Richland. He specialized in V-8 conversions. I dropped off my truck and a check in June. I drove my parent's Oldsmobile Cutlass Supreme in the interim.

For four months I obsessed over my truck. I dreamt about it. I bragged about it. I made it a main topic in many conversations. I called the guy almost every weekend and asked for updates. I drove back and forth to Richland on many weekends to check the progress. But he procrastinated on the project. He made excuse after excuse for the delay.

Each day passed and my impatience increased. Fall arrived and I gave him an ultimatum. I drove to Richland to pick up my truck. I discovered he only finished about 80-percent of the conversion.

He hadn't installed the speedometer. The reverse lights weren't connected. My truck didn't have a catalytic converter (illegal). Disbelief and frustration overwhelmed me. I didn't want to deal with the situation any longer. I wanted my hot-rod truck.

Then I started my truck for the first time. My jaw dropped. The growl of the engine and the exhaust note astonished me. The rumble from inside the cab excited me. I roasted the tires on my first test drive. I temporarily forgot about the four months of frustration I experienced.

I drove my truck back to Seattle. Exhilaration seeped from my pores. High on excitement, I put new rims and tires on my truck. I painted it. I installed a new stereo system. My friends wanted rides in my truck. I volunteered to drive my truck for almost any reason.

But after a couple months my high subsided. The original problems with my truck plagued me. New problems were a thorn in my side. The starter often locked up. I popped the hood, tapped on it with a metal bar, and started the truck. I repeated the routine almost daily. My truck also ran hot with an inadequate cooling fan. Many times I pulled over and popped the hood. I waited fifteen to twenty minutes for the engine to cool down.

I averaged about ten miles per gallon. My gas and rent expenses were almost equal. My truck became more and more of a hassle to own. The joy of my truck turned into irritation and frustration.

But I didn't want to get rid of it. I had invested so much time, effort, and energy. But one experience brought finality to the hope I put in my truck.

The oil pressure, engine temperature, and voltage gauges were together. They were installed on a small shelf under the dashboard. A white tube led from behind the oil pressure gauge to the engine block. I stopped at a red light near my apartment and I reached under the shelf to grab some loose change. I accidentally hooked the oil pressure tube with my finger and I pulled it off the back of the oil gauge.

The light turned green. I pushed the gas pedal down and hot oil squirted into my cab. I panicked. I pushed the gas pedal down more to get out of the intersection. More and more hot oil squirted into the cab. I pulled over near my apartment. I had burned my hands. Oil flooded my cab and my truck stunk. My pants and shoes were destroyed.

I sold my truck a few weeks later. I invested about $12,000 into the truck and sold it for $3,200. I reaped more frustration and expense than joy and excitement. My obsession with the truck increased the void in my heart. My pursuit to find identity and value in a muscle car failed miserably. My truck offered no substance of hope or remedy to my heartache.

My twenty-third year wound down. The college persona and swagger continued to fade. I went to Cheney for Thanksgiving. While there I got my second tattoo under my left bicep. An image of three strong arms locked together forming a peace sign. The words "United We Stand, Divided We Fall" encircle the peace sign.

I dedicated the tattoo to my friends and family in the military. I needed a way to acknowledge the significance of their sacrifice. I also used the tattoo to punish myself with guilt. Guilt for being alive when men and women were dying for my country.

In addition, my tattoo demonstrated my loyalty towards my friends I considered brothers. I visited some of my brothers in Cheney. While there I hung out a few times on the Eastern campus. I tried to act grown up and professional.

I puffed up with pride with my cell phone in my belt holder. I handled a few business calls in the PUB. I annoyed people. I embarrassed some of my friends. Strangers looked at me as an outsider.

I still held onto a glimmer of hope from my former college life. I thought my visit would somehow resuscitate it. I sat on the sitting wall in front of the PUB like old times. But I didn't recognize anyone. I didn't high five students or play card games.

I strolled through my old dorm and visited the athletic center. In private, I knelt down and laid my hands on the campus and it invoked an avalanche of memories. I shed tears as I smelled familiar smells and heard familiar sounds.

I went to Outback Jack's the last night of my visit. I walked in disillusioned and sat near the dance floor. Out of place and disconnected, the experience crushed me. I ended the night hollow.

Eastern moved on without me. I realized the finality of my visit. My glory days were over.

CHAPTER THIRTEEN

Finally, Love

I RETURNED TO my life in western Washington. Around March 1999 I moved to a sketchy part of Renton, Washington. I rented the bottom level of a duplex with a friend and his co-worker. It was an undesirable but affordable option. A family of palm-reader gypsies lived upstairs. The duplex was less than fifteen miles from my office in Auburn.

Low self-esteem left me vulnerable to female attention. My active radar constantly scanned for female compliments. The small alarm company staff frequently hung out together. I developed a genuine platonic friendship with a sales guy and his wife.

I subtly flirted with her on different occasions. Her return signals motivated me. The couple invited me to a party at their home one summer night. In my element, I showed off. Uninhibited, my flirtatious mannerisms amplified. Toward the end of the night we messed around.

The next morning she called me. We admitted our mistake. I disregarded their marriage for my own selfish gain. I broke my friend's trust. My friendship faded with the couple. The void in my heart enlarged. Flashbacks of ruined high school friendships haunted me.

My poor decision didn't deter me. I committed a repeat offense. Within six months I met an engaged girl through a mutual friendship. We became acquaintances with no romantic connection. We socialized together in group gatherings. But, over the course of three months, we flirted a few times.

One night she called me and expressed frustration with her fiancé. She wanted to vent face to face. I invited her to my place. We drank several cocktails. She hinted of a fantasy to be married to me. A few hours later we slept together.

The next day guilt and shame suffocated me. My morals had hit an all-time low. My desperation for love and attention smothered the sense to do right. Our friendship ended. Emptiness burrowed deeper into my heart.

My life began to tailspin. In July 1999 I quit my job. I quit without a plan and had saved little money. A month later Southwest Airlines hired me as a ramp agent. I trained for two weeks. I lacked the necessary skills and quit the first day out of training.

Unemployment wrecked me. I lost confidence to look for new jobs. I stayed awake most nights until 3:00 a.m. I rarely woke up before noon. I vegged on the couch and binged on TV.

I ate poorly and didn't exercise. I stopped investing time in sermons and TBN. My bank account dwindled. I took out a loan at 26-percent interest to pay rent and daily expenses. I repeated the cycle of lethargy for four months. I bankrupted myself physically, spiritually, and emotionally.

But, in my darkest times, Jesus never left me. He reminded me of His love in unique ways. In August 1999 I went on my annual Wallowa Lake camping trip. Oregon was experiencing a moderate drought and the water levels in the lake were below normal.

High overcast clouds and a thick haze blanketed the ninety-plus degree day. My friends and I walked out about one hundred yards into the lake. A dead carp floated in the water. I picked it up and threw it at my friend. A war game of mud and rocks ensued.

In the excitement of our game, the Holy Spirit stopped me. He turned my attention to the side of a nearby mountain. I gazed at a green patch of grass several hundred feet in diameter. A giant sun ray blasted through a gap in the haze. It lit up the green patch.

Here I am, He said. God arrested my heart.

I turned and shouted to my friends, "Look, guys, look up there. What do you see?"

They responded, "What? Oh yeah, I see the light. That's cool."

"No, that's GOD," I proclaimed.

Jesus resuscitated my life. I returned to Renton revitalized. My friend's parents from Kennewick came to visit. Their daughter Lola accompanied them. I said to my friend, "I didn't know you had a sister." I introduced myself.

Lola inquired about jobs in western Washington. My friend worked for Horizon Airlines. He convinced her to get a job there. A few weeks later she moved into the duplex. With three roommates already, Lola shared a room with her brother.

I helped her acclimate to the area. I cooked breakfast for her and my roommates almost daily. I offered Lola rides to and from work. I hid my attraction from her. Our five-and-a-half year age difference made things awkward. I also didn't know how her brother would react.

By mid-September I couldn't hide my feelings any longer. I dropped small hints to her. My attempts fell woefully short. I didn't receive the adoration I hoped. She dismissed my efforts to woo her. In addition, I found myself among competition. Some of Lola's male co-workers were attracted to her. And a few of her past relationships caught up with her.

Jealousy snuffed out my confidence. My insecurities and inadequacies flared up. Jealousy and unemployment created a toxic mixture. *See, it's not worth it. Why would she want me? I'll never get married. I'll be alone forever,* I thought.

I wallowed in my misery. I detested living under the palm readers. I drank often. I lost about thirty pounds. People remarked about my emaciated figure. I hated my life.

But I endured the storms of my mind. I fought through the drama of life. I continued to pursue Lola. Eventually, she came to her senses. She stopped resisting me. She started to like me.

We hung out together more and more. I did various things to impress her. I spent money on her I didn't have. We asked her brother for permission to date. He privately said to Lola, "I am worried about you dating Bill. He never takes anything seriously." Other friends and family reacted with trepidation. They weren't sure whether to congratulate us or reprimand us.

We officially became an item in early October. For a month and a half we were rarely apart. In November of 1999, her brother married in the Tri-Cities. I emceed the wedding. We stepped outside of the reception to get some fresh air. Lola turned to me. "Bill, I love you."

My ears exploded. "You do? I didn't know you felt that way. But I love you too." My heart pounded like the twelfth man inside my chest. I longed to hear her say she loved me.

I drove back to Renton in a euphoric and invincible state. We remained in the puppy love stage for the next couple months. Lola eventually moved into my room. My outlook on life became positive.

I kick-started a new career. AT&T hired me as a customer care rep in January 2000. A steady job and source of income made me feel productive again. Depending on my shift, my commute averaged one and a half to two hours each way. I listened to sermons on the radio again. I watched TBN at home. I chased after Jesus with a new flare.

People in their early twenties dominated the call center culture. I fit in well. I acquired the necessary job skills quickly. The call center measured employees on a wide range of key performance indicators (KPIs). Shift bids, bonuses, and promotion opportunities were influenced by performance. I cared about those things. But performance meant more to me than dollar signs and promotions.

Performance equaled personal value. I consistently performed above expectations. Many times I received perfect scores in all the measured categories. I received compliments like, "You did an outstanding job." "You are leading the team in this area."

But I dismissed my success. I didn't celebrate a 100-percent score. I demanded perfection at minimum; anything less equaled failure. I sought out mistakes. I used them to substantiate my worthlessness. I asked my supervisors, "But what about my mistakes? I want to know what I am doing wrong."

I attributed perfection to value and worth. My impossible standard of perfection made it impossible for me to feel valued. My unhealthy formula of value created a distorted view of recognition. I abhorred rewards and recognition. Compliments insulted me. I focused on my failures for punishment.

Each quarter employees nominated other employees for the Spirit of Excellence (SOE) award. A committee reviewed all the nominations. They selected a handful to receive the award. Winners received monetary prizes and other goodies.

Then, once a year the same committee reviewed all the SOE winners. They selected a handful to receive the Circle of Excellence (COE) award, the highest recognition in the company. The award included a one-week fully-paid trip to the Hilton Waikoloa Village in Kona, Hawaii.

Towards the end of March I attended my first all-hands meeting. COE awards were announced. I envied the winners on stage. I hung my head and thought, *I could never win an award like that. I will never be up there. There are a number of talented and smart people in this company. I am just another employee.*

Jesus disagreed. Over the course of eight years I worked hard. Driven by passion and dedication. I received six SOE nominations and two COE nominations. I won the SOE award four times and COE one time.

By March, Lola and I had dated for about six months. The puppy love stage wore off. We faced real challenges in our relationship. Our immaturity and naivety surfaced. Our past baggage and issues caught up to us. We argued. We fought. The perfect relationship I envisioned croaked. We made a poor decision to live together. It created additional stress.

In summer 2000 I moved into an apartment in Renton, Washington. I lived with a different friend from college. Lola moved to Federal Way with a friend. Her parents also moved to Federal Way from Kennewick. We clung to our bad habits. Most of the time she stayed with me.

We grew closer together. But our faults and weaknesses created ongoing tension. We resented each other for various things in our lives. We struggled with jealousy. Her Catholic background clashed with my radio and television church background.

I resorted to my old vow and safety zone. *Don't let her get too close. You know the rule.* I pulled away from her and became distant. Our relationship flatlined.

Lola called me one evening in the fall. The conversation started poorly. Twenty minutes into the conversation she asked, "Do you want to break up with me?" I paused for several seconds. I engaged in a shouting match in my mind.

Let her go, you don't need her. She doesn't love you.

No. Don't let her go, you love her too much.

I realized my actions originated from a place of fear—fear of commitment. My defense mechanism told me to leave her before she hurt me. But I refused to continue the cycle. I responded to her in a calm and relaxed voice, "No, babe, I don't want to break up with you. I love you. Come over."

Our phone conversation changed the course of my future.

CHAPTER FOURTEEN

Total Rejection

WE DECIDED NOT to quit on each other. I depended on her love and support. But the void in my heart enlarged. About a year into our relationship I picked up gambling. Initially, casinos seemed like harmless entertainment. My roommate from my freshman year in college accompanied me often.

But the "for fun" activity turned into an addiction. Gambling consumed my time. I frequented a casino next to my apartment. Six to eight hours on Fridays and Saturdays became the norm. I drank and gambled. I told jokes and stories. I nursed on the reactions from other gamblers and dealers.

My first-name basis with fellow gamblers instilled a false sense of importance. I justified my actions by claiming people needed me there. Disillusioned and in denial, I scoffed at the mention of an addiction.

I ignored good-willed warnings from dealers to stop. I visited the cash machine many times. I withdrew cash from my credit card account. Red and green chips melted my bank account. My health declined again. I became lethargic.

My emotional and physical absence strained my relationship with Lola. But we continued dating and our relationship intensified.

The topic of marriage came up a few times in conversations. We joked and hinted with friends about the potential of marriage. My heart wanted a lifelong companion. But my head feared it.

In fall 2001 I moved into a one-bedroom apartment in Mill Creek, Washington. My commute reduced to twenty minutes. Lola moved in with me. My career progressed. My consistent performance at work earned me a few promotions. I leveled up within the ranks of call center support.

By then I had won a few SOE awards. I established a reputation as a go-to guy in the call center. The attention appeared glamourous. People relied on me. I loved my job. I wallowed less in the muck and mire of my life. My new outlook inspired me to take a bold step. I decided to ask Lola to marry me.

I desired for the moment to be romantic and memorable. I sought her dad's permission first. But I didn't have a well-thought-out plan. I chose to pop the question on Christmas Eve.

We ate dinner at Lola's parent's apartment. My mind stayed distracted the entire time. I looked for an opportunity to be alone with her dad. The moment came when he prepared to take the garbage outside.

I said, "Oh, I'll help you with that." I carried a few garbage bags with him. I skipped the small talk. "You know, I have been dating your daughter for a while now and I love her. And . . . well . . . I was wondering if I could have your permission to marry her?"

We arrived at the giant garbage receptacle. The scene hit me. *Did I really just ask my future father-in-law for permission to marry his daughter while taking the garbage out?* I worried about the lack of honor I portrayed. My lame effort wasn't eloquent at all. But his receptiveness surprised me. "I see that you treat my daughter well and have a good heart. You have my permission."

We walked back into the apartment. I concealed my elation. About an hour later Lola and I left the apartment. I told her I wanted to drive through downtown Seattle. I invented a fictitious story about a huge Christmas event.

She put me on the spot. "What Christmas event?"

I responded, "Oh, I can't give you too many details. It's a surprise." We drove towards Seattle. I panicked. *Where am I going to go? What am I going to do?"* I wanted to propose to her somewhere downtown near Christmas lights. But I didn't know where.

We exited downtown. I crept through the streets. I said, "The Christmas event is around here somewhere." But the streets were empty. The stores and shops were closed. There were no signs of activity or events.

Lola questioned me. "Are you sure it's around here?"

"Yes, yes, just trust me" I answered.

I saw the Harbor Steps in my peripheral vision. I parked the car. "We need to walk up the steps because I think the party is up there." Lola didn't believe me but played along.

We walked up a few steps. I stopped her next to the water fountain. The lights reflected beautifully off the water. She asked, "Wait, what's going on?"

I gulped. I got on my knee. I proposed to her.

"I knew there wasn't a Christmas event," she said, giggling.

Despite the joy and exhilaration of my engagement, trouble lingered in my mind. I doubted my decision. I still feared the commitment. I wrestled with my vow. "Bill, you made a promise. You said you would *never* get married."

I hoped the uneasiness of my decision would melt away before the wedding. I couldn't escape the memories of my failed engagement from college. I questioned my motives for asking Lola to marry me.

For the next nine months we (Lola) planned our wedding. We decided to marry in the Catholic church. With no church history I couldn't rebut. But I knew the tradition meant a lot to Lola and her family. I respected their wishes.

I was young and naïve. My thoughts were centered on having a successful wedding ceremony, not a lifelong commitment to Lola. I focused my efforts on impressing my family and friends.

There were fourteen people in our wedding party. I invited five groomsmen and four ushers to stand with me. Most were the friends I considered brothers. Lola struggled to invite enough bridesmaids to match my groomsmen.

My groomsmen and ushers gathered in the basement of the church. We changed into our tuxes. We laughed and reminisced. I paused to soak in the moment. I looked at them and thought, *Here are all of my friends in one place. A dream I longed to come true.*

I considered the moment the pinnacle of loyalty. At the same time my heart sank. I stated, "I know after this wedding ceremony, our friendship will never be the same again. I knew this was the last time I would be with my friends like that again.

The guys headed upstairs for pictures. Lola prepared herself in a different room in the church. I stood a few feet from the entrance to her room. She stepped out of the room. Our eyes locked. She took my breath away. Her eyes and smile sparkled in her beautiful wedding dress.

My heart burst with joy. *Wow, that's my bride.* We met face to face. I whispered, "You are so beautiful." The comfort of our embrace erased all concerns about the future.

The ceremony began. I stood calm and composed when Lola walked down the aisle. The ceremony lasted about an hour and a half. Things proceeded smoothly. We were introduced to our friends and family as husband and wife. We threw our arms up and shouted, "We did it." Together we let out a big sigh of relief. We married in September 2002.

Many friends and family pitched in to support our special day. The reception hall looked like a professional masterpiece. The decorations were stunning. A friend of the family and restaurant owner catered the food. Almost three hundred people attended the wedding and reception.

We were blessed by all the love and support and we couldn't have asked for a better night. We honeymooned in Cabo San Lucas and we stayed in a timeshare condo on the beach. My brother and sister-in-law came along also.

Sadly, the wedding and honeymoon didn't cure my hopelessness. I exhibited my selfish tendencies. My single mindset dominated. I drank each night in Cabo. I went overboard one night. Intoxicated and obnoxious, I treated my bride and in-laws with contempt. I treated our honeymoon like a weekend getaway, like a random night on the town. I didn't honor Lola like she deserved.

We struggled in the first couple years of our marriage. My old habits and baggage raged against Lola's old habits and baggage. I didn't understand the concept of a committed life. Living together before we married compounded our issues.

Not much changed in my selfish behavior. I frequented casinos. I lost thousands of dollars. I drank often on the weekends. I acted belligerent one night on our way home from a party. I argued about something ridiculous. Lola put her hand on my arm. She told me to calm down. I grabbed her arm and squeezed hard. She winced in pain. "Ouch. Bill let go; you are hurting me." I squeezed for a few seconds more before letting go.

I woke up horrified the next morning. I crumpled under the guilt and shame of my actions. I realized what I was capable of. I saw a monster in me. I descended into one of the deepest valleys in my marriage. Lola forgave me, but I didn't.

Life continued on. We moved into a two-bedroom apartment in the same complex. Lola enrolled in the Gene Juarez Beauty Academy. She attended all-day classes between Tuesdays and Saturdays. Our long periods of time apart drove a wedge in our marriage. I lived a separate individual life. For a period of time we were married roommates.

We knew we needed to change. We wanted to be part of a church together. We couldn't figure out how to meet on common ground. Her Catholic background and my unchurched radio ministry collided.

We attended a Foursquare church in Mill Creek for a handful of months. We liked the pastors. Powerful messages and engaging worship attracted us. We met a few couples. They genuinely welcomed us. They made efforts to invite us to different events and activities.

But I remained leery of organized church. I believed I didn't need to attend. I survived growing up without church. Besides, radio and television ministry satisfied my need. I declined invites to hang out with people from Foursquare. I remained loyal to my promise not to make any more friends. My friendship switch remained off.

Lola responded differently. She involved herself in events and activities. She longed to be connected. Lola's heart changed. God began a work in her.

My absence made things difficult for Lola. She provided excuses on my behalf for my lack of attendance. Her relationship with Jesus blossomed. I resisted His love. My search for purpose and identity continued.

I supposed the military offered them. The persona of the military intrigued me. I blurred the lines of fascination and obsession for the military. I watched movies like *Blackhawk Down*, *We Were Soldiers* and *Saving Private Ryan*. Heroism and valor exploded on the screen. I wanted to be a hero and mighty man of valor.

I wanted to experience the bond of brotherhood that can only be found in the military. I wanted to know the camaraderie shared in a foxhole. I want to know the allegiance created during the chaos of a firefight. The closest bond I ever created was with my teammates on the soccer field.

I often grilled family and friends about their experiences in the military. I asked questions like, "What's it like to get ambushed?"

"Did you ever call for air support?" "What formations and tactics did you use when clearing buildings or advancing on positions?"

I elevated people in the military above civilians. I justified my logic based on suffering, sacrifice, and the hardships of war. Guilt inundated my thoughts for not serving in the military. My grandpa served in the Navy in WW II. He experienced horrific things while on Iwo Jima for thirteen months. My father-in-law served in Vietnam. He also experienced terrible things while manning howitzers on a firebase.

My career seemed inadequate compared to their sacrifice. I believed, *If I could just be like them then I would have purpose in my life.* I wanted to be a hero like Dave Roever. I seriously considered joining the military. I considered the chief warrant officer rank to fly Black Hawk helicopters. I also envisioned being a second lieutenant in the infantry. But my wife and family urged me not to join.

I abandoned efforts to pursue a military career. But I advanced in my AT&T career. I promoted to customer care trainer in March 2004. I shifted from talking to customers to teaching classes of twenty-five to thirty employees. Classes lasted eight hours a day. They rotated every six to eight weeks.

A perfect fit for my communication degree. My natural gifts for speaking shone. I developed a strong passion to teach. I devoted myself to the role of trainer. I worked hard to create a focused but fun environment. I invented games. I wove in fun stories to break up the information overload. The well-being and success of each new hire became my personal mission. I didn't mind long hours and one-on-one time.

I easily developed rapport with the new hires. I established a good reputation within the training department. Trainers were evaluated on a number of classroom related performance indicators. Results and feedback from surveys were critical for me.

Positive feedback validated me. It gave me a sense of euphoria. I fed on comments like, "You are our favorite trainer," "We have so much fun in your class," or "Bill, you are super knowledgeable and I learn so much from you."

But I did not allow myself to be fooled. I demanded perfection at minimum. I didn't want to give into deceptive thoughts of I did a good job. I hunted through feedback for negative comments. I needed to find mistakes to validate my worthlessness.

If a new hire didn't pass the final I blamed myself. I convinced myself I didn't do enough. I didn't teach well enough. I didn't articulate clearly enough. Co-workers posted positive feedback and recognition on their desks. I refused to display mine. I stored positive feedback in boxes. I displayed negative ones to remind myself of my mistakes.

But my view of value and validation didn't align with God's. I believed the output of the work of my hands equaled value. I thought He only loved me based on performance. I thought I could only earn His love through perfection.

But Jesus taught me otherwise. I couldn't earn His love. He just gave it to me. My work performance didn't persuade Him. He saw past my faults as a husband. He didn't tremble from my gambling addiction. He didn't run from my drinking habits.

He offered me hope. But I rejected it. I didn't listen.

CHAPTER FIFTEEN

I Ignored Jesus—Again

IN JANUARY 2005 Lola and I looked to buy our first home. Housing prices close to the call center were exceptionally high. Our budget limited our choices to old and small homes. We expanded our search much farther north. Much newer homes in our price range were available in Lake Stevens, Washington.

We drove to a neighborhood one afternoon. I instantly found a home I liked. "This is exactly the house I want, in the location I want, in the neighborhood I want," I said. The housing market peaked during our search. Homes sold within twenty-four hours of being listed on MLS.

We called our realtor, my sister-in-law. The house had sold by the time she looked it up. We experienced the same results several more times. Dismayed and discouraged, I almost gave up. I conceded, "Who am I kidding? I'll never get the house I want. It's impossible. Why dream for a home I want when I'll just end up disappointed?"

A few days later our realtor called. "A house in that exact area you were looking is about to come on the market in a few hours. I'll meet you up there, so get ready to make an offer." I taught a class so I couldn't go. But Lola drove up to Lake Stevens to meet her.

Lola walked through the house and then called me. I saw the photos online. I asked, "What's it like? Do you like it? Should we get it?"

She trembled in her response. "I don't know. I like it but I don't know if it's the right one. I have never done this before. I feel overwhelmed."

At the time I didn't understand the enormity of the situation. A tremendous responsibility rested on Lola's shoulders. But because of the aggressive market we made an offer after our phone conversation.

We had less than $2,000 as a down payment. A weak offer. Our realtor left the home to write up an offer. She called a few minutes later. "Wow. Since the time we looked at the house and began the paperwork there are already four offers on the house. One offer includes $40,000 cash down." In the meantime, our realtor forgot some additional paperwork at the house. She drove back to retrieve it. The current homeowners arrived at the same time.

My sister-in-law was pregnant at the time with our niece. Her pregnancy sparked a conversation with the homeowners. They chatted for about a half hour. My sister-in-law explained our situation. The family enjoyed the conversation and liked our story. They accepted our $2,000 offer despite the much stronger $40,000 offer.

In February 2005 God blessed us with our first home.

I recognized the purchase of our home wasn't a coincidence. I knew God orchestrated the miracle. Through our experience, Jesus reminded me of His goodness. He once again demonstrated His love for me. He gently communicated, *Why do you doubt me? I am always faithful.*

The location only increased my commute by fifteen minutes. I continued to excel in my trainer role. Lola graduated Gene Juarez Beauty Academy and her advanced training courses. Her career kicked off at the Gene Juarez salon in Lynnwood.

We had accumulated several thousand dollars of debt from our wedding and school loans. But, from a vocation perspective, our lives were comfortable. In our DINK (dual-income, no kids) lifestyle, we spent money without a concept of a budget and ate at restaurants several times a month. We went out often and didn't save money. If only we knew about Dave Ramsey.

From a marriage perspective we were broke. Lola worked most weekends. I had weekends off. Our opposite schedules drove us apart. We didn't invest in our marriage. We didn't work towards intimacy. We lived individual lives.

The absence of Lola distracted me. I exploited my alone time. My exploration lead me to the world of online pornography. High-speed Internet enabled quick and easy access.

I dabbled in pornography a few times here and there. But the lust and lure ensnared me. Pornography crept into my life. I didn't have the discipline or support to stop. I soon engaged several times a week. Similar to my gambling addiction, I became disillusioned. I didn't view pornography as an addiction. I knew the filth it represented, but my desire for pleasure overruled my conscience.

To mitigate my sin I created guidelines. I convinced myself boundaries would make my behavior acceptable. I created rules. I could only look at pornography a certain amount of time each day. I promised to never spend money on it. Free sites were justifiable.

The snares and traps I set for myself drew me in more. My efforts to manage my sin failed miserably. My "rules" and "guidelines" vanished. I no longer followed my allotted time slots. I spent money on different sites. I nosedived in my feeble willpower.

I paid for digital sex. I engaged in digital prostitution. Pornography perverted intimacy with Lola. It created more stress. It stunted growth in our marriage. Soon a canyon in our relationship developed.

But I didn't stop. My vulnerable mind left me susceptible to unchecked and unfiltered thoughts. I used the classroom platform to flirt. Each new class presented opportunities for me to show off. I impressed and gained the admiration of females.

Girls noticed me. They smiled at me. They laughed at my stories. They gave me compliments in the hallways. I wasn't disciplined with the attention. I liked the attention. I had no desire to stop the behavior. I ignored feelings of infidelity towards my wife.

Those feelings propelled me towards another form of flirtation. I rediscovered the world of online chatting. Similar to pornography, I started slowly. I chatted a few times. But I quickly became engrossed. And I didn't reenact my college day chats. Instead, I learned to flirt with strangers.

One-on-one conversations with strangers seemed unusual at first. Again, I tried to implement rules and guidelines. I promised to never meet the women I flirted with. I promised to never be physically involved with another woman.

I sought out women from states far away. I especially looked for women in different countries. I wanted to be faithful to my rules. Women gave me compliments and validated me. Their expressed desire for me made me feel attractive. I fed on compliments from strange women. I relied on them to maintain my self-esteem.

I learned illicit chat techniques. Words on a screen progressed to photo sharing. Photo sharing escalated to videos. I became promiscuous online. I convinced myself I wasn't committing adultery. I believed digital sex was not real sex. I didn't actually sleep with anyone. I didn't get a girl pregnant. I didn't catch or spread an STD. I chalked it up as harmless satisfaction and fun.

Lola knew about my pornography addiction. But I kept chatting a secret. My behavior didn't go unnoticed by Jesus. Many times He confronted my behavior. He challenged me to deal with my sin. He made my gut wrench on several occasions. But I ignored Him.

One day while I watched TBN, Jesse Duplantis preached a sermon on sin. In his sermon he said, "You know why you sin?

Because you don't hate it. You hate the consequences of sin. You hate how it makes you feel afterwards. But you don't hate sin."

Jesse's message floored me. I knew Jesus wanted me to hear it. I never experienced condemnation by Jesus. But I clearly knew how my behavior hurt His heart.

Despite the Lord's clear warning, pornography and online chatting continued.

CHAPTER SIXTEEN

Changed

B UT JESUS NEVER gave up on me. His plan for my life
didn't cease because of my brokenness. Jesus operated
behind the scenes for years. In late 2004 He brought Pastor
Aaron into my life.

I first met Pastor Aaron in the call center. We talked often over
the course of several months. We bragged about God. We boasted
on the Bible. Our conversations encouraged me. His passion for
Jesus excited me. I marveled at his wisdom and knowledge about
the Word. He taught me things I didn't know.

In early 2005 Pastor Aaron made a profound declaration. "Hey
Bill, I am going to start my own church." My heart leapt inside my
chest. I responded with excitement and joy. I committed to the
church the moment he uttered his declaration. A few weeks later
I wrote him a $100 check. My first official tithe with a purpose.

He didn't set a firm date. I pestered him for about a month.
"When are you going to start the church?" One day he set a launch
date in March. I attended my first Connection Point Church service
in the PUD building in Everett, Washington. My life in the body
of Christ began.

I eagerly awaited the arrival of each Sunday. A profound hunger to be connected to the body of Christ radiated in me. The dormant spiritual DNA inside me awakened. I dedicated myself to each Sunday. The small church alleviated worries of my unchurched background. Knowing Pastor Aaron provided comfort and safety.

I didn't know the proper flow of service. I wasn't versed on church etiquette. But passion to know more about Jesus burned inside me. I served in ways I knew how. I helped set up the equipment, arrange the chairs and prepare for service.

For the first six months Lola and I couldn't attend church together. She worked at the salon on Sundays. But her schedule changed. God poured into our hearts together at Connection Point Church. I sold out for Jesus. A much different attitude compared to when I attended Foursquare.

Lola and I thrived in our new church home and we adjusted to the change. She struggled internally going to a non-Catholic church. Her choice introduced a new dynamic to her parents and extended family.

But, overtime, Lola's strong ties to her Catholic background faded. I rescinded my previous stance that I only needed radio and television ministry. I soaked up my new church life like a sponge.

Connection Point eventually moved from the PUD building to a grade-school cafeteria. We set up and tore down the sound equipment, chairs, and tables each Sunday. Pastor Aaron's sermons refreshed me. I habitually read God's Word. The more I read, the more He revealed Himself to me. The Bible fascinated me. I kicked myself. *Why did I ignore this book my whole life?* Dr. Adrian Rogers said in one of his Adrianisms, "When there is dust on Bible there is drought in the heart."

Tremendous growth happened in my life within the first year at Connection Point Church. By spring 2006 I matured more in my faith. Then Pastor Aaron dropped a bomb on me. One Sunday before service he came up to me privately. He said, "Hey, in a couple weeks I want you to open my sermon by speaking for five minutes or so." Insert the sound of a record being scratched. *You want me to do what?* I shouted in my mind.

I agreed to do it on the spot. I wanted to make Pastor Aaron proud. But I trembled inside. Not a big deal for me to speak for five minutes in front of a congregation of less than twenty. But a huge deal because of the "open-my-sermon" part. Why? I considered myself unworthy. A wretched and unlovable loser. An adulterer. A glutton for alcohol. A disgrace to the pulpit.

I wrestled with my mind for a week. Do I dare speak God's Word when I am not qualified? I appreciated my role in the congregation. I never thought I would be speaking in front of them. But, I prepared my five-minute opening to Pastor Aaron's sermon. I hand wrote it on a piece of notebook paper.

Fire didn't fall from heaven. The Holy Spirit didn't break out. But I did the best I could. I brimmed with contentment. Lola congratulated me. A patterned developed. Pastor Aaron asked me to open for him again a few weeks later. But for ten minutes. A few weeks later, fifteen minutes. By summer I regularly opened sermons for Pastor Aaron.

Then the unthinkable happened. He asked me to preach an entire sermon. By myself. I withered like a contestant on *Fear Factor*. Blindfolded and forced to reach into a bucket of creepy crawlies. But again, I said yes. I invested quality time into preparing the sermon. I memorized most of it. I rehearsed out loud. I almost fainted the Saturday night before service.

On Sunday I preached to the best of my ability. My church family applauded. I walked back to my seat. Pastor Aaron stood in front of the church. With emotion he spoke, "The Lord has shown me that you have a heart of gold. I would take a bullet for you, my friend." From then on I knew the Lord had my back. He prepared me for things I never knew were possible.

Over the course of the next year Pastor Aaron taught me to preach and study. He mentored me. I likened our relationship to Paul and Timothy. He introduced me to the Holy Spirit. He explained the power and importance of prayer. He spoke prophetic words over me. He shared dreams and visions the Lord gave Him about me. He opened my eyes to the supernatural and prophetic realm.

I learned about people like Jonathan Welton and Sid Roth. Pastor Aaron baptized me and Lola in Lake Stevens. I learned more about the knowledge and wisdom of God. Church cultivated an attitude of intimacy with me and Jesus.

In 2008 Pastor Aaron approached me before service. "It's time to commission you as our associate pastor." I reacted with disbelief. I resisted the title. *Not me, do you know who I am? Do you know about my garbage? I am not a pastor. I don't have a seminary degree in theology. I am not versed in Jewish history. I didn't grow up in church.*

I compared myself to the prestigious pastors I listened to on the radio and television. My miniscule existence disappeared in the shadows of Billy Graham, Dr. Charles Stanley and Bishop T.D. Jakes. I couldn't even measure up to Pastor Aaron.

I put God in a box. I reduced His power in my mind. I argued with Him. I gave Him many excuses why I should not have a title of associate pastor. *I don't have the talents and gifts so and so has. I don't have what it takes. I am not credentialed. I don't come from a family of preachers.*

Thankfully, Pastor Aaron pushed me out of my comfort zone. I gradually matured more and more in my relationship with Jesus. I invested my heart in His Word. I built a library of sermons and resources from radio and television ministry.

The more intimate I became with Jesus, the more He used me. But I repelled thoughts of my usefulness. My resistance steered me back to the Word. I studied the different men Jesus used in the Bible. Men who I shared similar doubts with.

Jesus showed me the doubt Moses and Gideon initially harbored. I found encouragement in *Twelve Unlikely Heroes* audio book by John MacArthur. God again showed me how He uses ordinary people to do extraordinary things. And my favorite, the blind man Jesus healed who challenged the religious leaders of the day (See John 9:1-41).

Jesus inundated me with additional examples of how He could use me. I learned from the DVD *Furious Love* how young kids teach and lead worship at Philip Mantofa's church. In Greg Laurie's *Parables from the Beach* DVD, he baptized a group of strangers as a new Christian. He had never baptized anyone before. He said, "I saw right there the power of the Gospel. I was not qualified. I really didn't have any training for it, but I felt like God would honor His word." I found encouragement through David Ring, an evangelist born with cerebral palsy and orphaned at age fourteen.

I watched an episode of Sid Roth's show, *It's Supernatural*. Rich Vera said something to the effect of: "So many young Christian leaders want to be like some of the great names like Oral Roberts and others. It's okay to admire them and like them but don't try to become them. If you try to become them, then your own growth and ministry will be limited. Not because those men and women aren't powerful, but God's will in their lives isn't His will in your life. Pursuing God's will for someone else's life in your life will be severely limiting. But pursuing God's will for your life will be unlimited in what He can do."

I told God, "Okay. I can't be Perry Stone. I can't be R.T. Kendall. I can't be Max Lucado. Help me to be who you created me to be."

I steadily lowered my wall of disbelief. I preached a sermon in late spring 2008. At the end I invited people to accept Jesus into their hearts. One lady in our church raised her hand. She came forward. We prayed for her and she gave her life to Jesus.

In the same year my brother accepted Jesus into his heart. He lived in South Carolina but we spoke on the phone often. During one conversation, the Holy Spirit led me to pray for my brother. He too gave His life to Jesus. The joy of their salvation changed my perspective. Resisting God became more difficult.

God changed Lola's heart too. She pursued intimacy with Jesus through worship. He revealed His heart to her through worship. Pastor Aaron asked Lola to be our worship leader. I didn't understand the power or significance of worship. I didn't understand the intimacy. I didn't know Jesus loves our worship. I glazed over scriptures like 1 Peter 1:12 and Luke 19:40.

My worship consisted of singing songs that elicited emotional reactions from me. But most of the reactions were rooted in guilt and condemnation. I stood with a defeated posture. My head hung low with my arms behind my back.

I didn't raise my hands. I kept my voice quiet. I didn't lean into worship for liberation and freedom. I thought, *How can I sing these words to you Lord? I am worthless. I cannot stand before you. I am wretched and full of sin.*

But Lola worshipped differently. Her spirit lit up despite her brokenness. She poured herself out to Jesus. She wasn't ashamed of her tears. She intrigued and inspired me. Lola invested in worship. She traveled to different worship conferences. She met people like Jonathan Lee and Hillsong United. Her faith grew through worship. Jesus transformed her.

I didn't experience the type of intimacy Lola experienced through worship. Fear and embarrassment hindered me. I didn't want people to hear me. I didn't want to stand out. I didn't want to be a weirdo.

But Lola's desire to seek God through worship affected me. God refined my heart. One day in church I made a decision. "I want to know *true* worship. I want what Lola has." We worshiped with the song "Fire Fall Down" from Hillsong United.

The song began. I stood in my usual posture. We reached the chorus. The Holy Spirit prompted me. I let go and surrendered. I lifted up both hands. I lifted up my head. Freedom and joy washed over me. Tears flowed down my face. Not from guilt and shame, but from the joy of worshipping Jesus.

Soon I listened to artists like Jason Upton, Deluge, and Hillsong United during my commute. My worship changed. Jesus changed me.

CHAPTER SEVENTEEN

The Truth and Nothing but the Painful Truth

THE YEARS BETWEEN 2006 and 2008 were filled with changes, growth, and challenges. Lola and I adopted a two-month-old black lab. Lola didn't grow up with pets. I hadn't had any since Cha Cha died. We learned how to adjust with Sasha in our lives.

We discovered Sasha's quirkiness when she was three months old. A few screws were loose in her head. She did inexplicable things but we loved her like a child. Friends and family adored her. We created many fun memories with her.

In January 2007 she turned one. I exercised her at a grade school near our home, a normal routine. The fenced-in grassy expanse provided the perfect play area. I jogged around the track and she explored the land.

About 6:30 p.m. we headed towards the parking lot. Sasha trotted ahead of me about twenty yards. She smelled the ground and wagged her tail. She paused halfway along the chain-link fence line and discovered a small switchback entrance she had never noticed before.

I sprinted towards her. "Sasha, no. Sasha, come," I yelled. She ignored me. She dashed through the fence. The school paralleled a busy main road. She trotted into the street oblivious to the traffic. A Toyota truck tried to stop in time.

The traumatic memory of my dog Skipper flashed before my eyes. Sasha tumbled underneath the truck. The sound of the impact reverberated in my ears. I cried out, "No, no, no, no! This cannot be happening." I launched into the middle of the street. I crumbled to my knees next to her.

She was motionless with a faint pulse when I picked her up. As I carried her to the sidewalk, I could tell many of her bones were broken. I laid her down and hurried to get my truck. Putting her in the back, I raced to the emergency vet's.

I called Lola on the way. When she answered, I could barely speak as I gave her the bad news. Lola met me at the emergency vet's and she cried when she saw Sasha in the back of my truck. The vets laid her on a cart and rushed her in. After a few minutes in the waiting area, a vet informed us, "She was too gravely wounded on the head. I am sorry; she is gone."

Breath vacated my lungs. We decided to cremate Sasha. The vets asked if we wanted to say goodbye one last time. Sasha lay on the examination table and I got on my knees in front of her. I wrapped my arms around her. Tears flowed down my face. I whispered, "I am so sorry, Sasha. I am so sorry. It's my fault, it's my fault."

Sasha's death choked the life out of me. Guilt and blame suffocated me. A torrent of sorrow flooded my mind. My world ended. I gave up. I sealed myself inside my spiritual Alcatraz.

Lola and I drove home stunned. We sat next to each other on the couch. Shock and disbelief kept us silent. I replayed the scene in my head. Lola withheld her emotions. She saw the devastation in my face. She held my hand and said, "I am worried about you."

Around 2:00 a.m., I lay on the couch and closed my eyes. I dreamt a vivid dream. I stood on the same sidewalk and street where Sasha died, but on a clear and bright day. I faced the sun.

The warmth lit up my face. Sasha ran up to me in her playful and unique way.

Filled with joy I thought, *I knew you were still alive. I knew this was just a bad dream.* I squatted down and embraced her. In the midst of the embrace I looked at her. I said, *Wait. No. Sasha, this is a dream. I know this isn't real. I watched you get hit by the truck and die.*

I stood up. A puddle of tears pooled at my feet. Sasha ran off and disappeared. When she did, God spoke to me. In a soft and sincere voice He said, *Bill, my grace is sufficient for you.* I instantly woke up. Peace washed over me. Indescribable warmth filled me. The life in His words flowed through my veins.

The tremendous guilt and blame for Sasha's death vanished. Jesus rescued me. He saved me from the abyss I almost jumped into. He didn't allow my life to be destroyed.

I shared my dream with Lola. Relief overwhelmed her. She knew I would not have recovered on my own. Through my experience, God taught me the difference between guilt and Holy Spirit conviction (See 2 Cor. 7:10). I listened to a sermon on guilt by R.T. Kendall. He said, "There are two kinds of guilt most of us will struggle with: true guilt (a result of our sin against God) and pseudo-guilt (when there is no sin in our lives)."

Kyle Idleman reinforced what I learned in his *Easter Experience* DVD series. He said, "Remorse is just an overwhelming regret that can turn you away from all hope. But repentance is when you let that regret turn you back to God." Six months after Sasha died we adopted another dog. Amber is a chocolate lab mix. She is a special part of our family.

May 2006 I applied for a new job: area manager, a highly-coveted position. The current employee put in his two week's notice. We had worked together on several projects and he suggested I apply.

The qualifications and expectations were beyond my experience. I replied, "Oh, thanks. But I think that role is for someone more qualified." He rebutted, "It won't hurt to try. I'll put in a good word for you."

Although intimidated, I applied, a huge leap of faith for me. I awaited an interview with trepidation. When I learned about the other candidates applying, my confidence dwindled even more. A week later the hiring manager scheduled an interview.

I answered his questions thoroughly and confidently. At the end of the interview I candidly said, "I have heard of the other candidates who applied. They are all very talented."

"Yes they are," he replied.

"I know I don't have the experience and am not as qualified as others, but I am willing to work hard and learn. I am teachable. How do people get these jobs anyway if they don't start somewhere? If I don't get this position how else will I ever get the experience and knowledge I need for this type of role?"

Two weeks later he called me back. "I was very impressed by your interview, especially our conversation at the end. I would like to offer you the position."

Word spread. The news shocked many people. I received congratulations from some people. But the majority murmured things like, "How did Bill get that job?" "Seriously, he's an area manager?" Some were downright appalled. They complained to the director and tried to appeal the decision.

By the end of summer people's concerns diminished. I had lived in western Washington nine years by then. I slowly lost touch with friends I made oaths with in high school and college—oaths like, "No matter what, when, where, how, or why, we will always be friends."

But time passed, distance increased and families grew. My declaration deteriorated. Each lost friendship ripped a hole in my heart. News of my best friend's divorce crushed me. He sold his house and moved to eastern Washington.

I helped him pack his things into a moving truck. We stood in his driveway one last time and I hugged him goodbye. "Thanks for always being there for me. Thanks for always being my friend." I knew our friendship would never be the same again. It never recovered. Hope in friendships vanished.

His departure solidified my decision; it was the final proof to weld my friendship switch in the off-position. I hardened my heart. For the next several years I barricaded myself from relationships.

However, I met two guys in the midst of my promise: one through soccer, the other the husband of my wife's friend. We eventually became friends and are still today. But I remained conflicted. I betrayed my friendship-switch vow. I disobeyed my rules.

Over the next year I matured in my role as area manager. I traveled often. I elevated my status and reputation, and became a go-to person for various projects. But my life changed when AT&T bought Cingular. As a result, I started a new career at T-Mobile in September 2007.

My commute increased to eighty miles round-trip. Drive time ranged between two and three hours. I used the time to grow in Jesus. I purchased various audio sermons. I listened to the Bible on audio CD—*The Bible Experience* for the Old Testament and *The Word of Promise* for the New Testament.

I preached one or two Sundays a month, but I struggled. My undisciplined mind bred harmful thoughts. I maintained suicidal thoughts and I viewed myself as worthless. I still didn't know my identity.

My pornography and chat addiction continued. By then, I knew Jesus' definition of adultery. He says in Matthew 5:27-28: "You have heard that it was said, 'You shall not commit adultery.' But I tell you that anyone who looks at a woman lustfully has already committed adultery with her in his heart."

I ignored His Word. I brushed aside the violation of covenant with my wife. I dismissed the women I lied to and used. The lust of physical gratification and attention overpowered purity. My actions were counterfeit to my walk with Jesus.

Lola eventually caught on. My gradual withdrawal from her became evident. My lack of intimacy manifested. I confessed. I broke her heart and I shattered her trust. My adulterous actions hurt Lola. I embarrassed her and I made her feel shameful.

Lola suffered from my infidelity. She competed for my love and physical attention and she shared me, neither of which she wanted to do. I sowed sexual sin into my life and I reaped a distorted sense of intimacy.

Lola struggled with my confession. She resented me. She harbored anger against me. I didn't blame her. I had failed her and betrayed her. I portrayed myself as the worst husband on the planet.

Overtime, the confession of my sin brought us closer together. We communicated more. We sought to understand each other better. We opened up more of our lives to each other. Breakthrough happened in our marriage.

But I kept my struggle a secret. I relapsed a few more times. I never confessed to anyone else. I never looked to someone I trusted to keep me accountable. My battle stayed behind closed doors.

CHAPTER EIGHTEEN

God's Blessings

I N FEBRUARY 2009 Lola and I attended a friend's wedding in California. We stayed with my parents. Lola didn't feel well the entire time. A pregnancy test confirmed her symptoms. We surprised my parents with the news first. Their outburst of elation damaged my eardrums. This would be their first grandchild. We told other family members and the joy and celebration continued.

Despite our excitement and eagerness, I remained in denial of the magnitude of bringing a child into our family. I dreaded my inadequacies and immaturity. I worried about failing my child. I didn't want my child to end up like me. I questioned God's decision to make me a dad. How could I be a father in my depravity?

For three quarters of my life I promised not to have kids. Now I carried the burden of an only grandchild in my family. I knew less than jack squat about pregnancy. Childbirth and babies were foreign to me. Lola grew up around babies and children. I rarely interacted with babies and children and avoided them. I chomped my fingernails until they looked like Orc nubs.

Lola researched information on pregnancy and birth. We elected to have a natural childbirth through a midwife. I encouraged

Lola as her body physically changed. I became accustomed to her protruding belly. I learned what to say and what not to say.

I participated in routine check-ups and doctor appointments. We shed tears of joy during our first sonogram. We saw our baby only a few centimeters long. Our baby leapt and did backflips in Lola's womb. My perspective changed. Around six months we determined the sex. It was a boy and I almost burst with pride.

I whispered to Jesus, "I am going to have a son." For about a month Lola and I enjoyed thinking of names. I suggested character names from some of my favorite movies. I lost. We wanted his name to have meaning. We chose the name Elijah from the Old Testament. We hoped for great things for our son. Elijah represented that.

Eight months into Lola's pregnancy she asked, "What are we going to do about your truck? How are we going to get a car seat in there?" The thought had never crossed my mind. I panicked. The same night I searched online for another car. I specifically wanted a sporty, four-door black truck with tinted windows. But my weak faith and God-in-a-box mentality doubted. *That's not possible. Jesus has more important things to do than get me a black truck.*

The next day my first online search returned a black 2005 Chevy Colorado. With tinted windows, sports package, low miles and within my price range. I laughed out loud. Less than two weeks later I parked the truck in my driveway. God delivered yet again. He gently reminded me, "Your house and truck was easy for me. How much more do you think I desire good things for you as a father?" (See Matt. 7:11).

The week of Lola's due date arrived and I appeared prepared and ready. I came home from work on a Monday expecting to have at least four or five more days. But thirty minutes later her contractions began. They began like small tremors, then changed into full-blown earthquakes.

I turned pale. Go time. I rushed to the grocery store and grabbed overnight supplies. Checkout seemed like eternity. We raced to the birthing center.

Labor progressed smoothly and the delivery was successful. Eleven hours later Lola laid Elijah on her chest and shoulder. I saw him for the first time. My heart fluttered. The reality of a new life hit me.

I hesitantly cut the umbilical cord. Elijah was born healthy and whole. But Lola's placenta didn't fully detach after birth. The midwife helped detach it, but, in the process, something happened.

She bled profusely. The atmosphere quickly changed. Celebration turned to concern. Lola's face turned white. She slipped towards unconsciousness. She looked towards the end of the bed. She pointed, "Who is that standing there at the end of the bed?"

Not a good sign. Fear swallowed me. For a few minutes I worried, *What is happening? This isn't supposed to happen. I can't lose my wife. How will I raise my son without her?* Within a few minutes the midwife stopped the bleeding, but Lola lost a lot of blood.

The event physically depleted her for a couple months. She lacked energy and stamina. The experience drew me closer to my wife. I appreciated the beauty and fragility of life. Despite the trauma, Jesus reminded me of His goodness. He pointed me to Pastor Louie Giglio's *Passion Talk* Series. In spite of my circumstances, He portrayed His love for me.

Elijah brought joy and light into our family. Our lives adapted and changed. We embraced new schedules and routines. My family and coworkers loved and supported us. Jesus refined my selfishness. He helped me get my eyes off myself. I learned how to be a dad. I learned how to survive on little sleep. I learned baby jargon. I developed diaper-changing skills. My gag reflex increased. I mastered swaddling techniques. Trips to the store no longer took a few minutes.

We chose to avoid daycare. I didn't want Lola working full-time just to pay for it. Elijah turned six months old. Lola went back to work part-time in a salon. When I came home from work Lola left for the salon. She pumped milk each day. We passed each other at night. The routine drained us.

Elijah turned one. Lola became a full-time stay-at-home mom. The decision came with difficulty. A mortgage and credit card debt exhausted our finances. We lived paycheck to paycheck. I noticed many moms with full time careers at T-Mobile. I became envious of the income. I wanted a fancy car. I wanted a big house. I wanted to go on vacations. I struggled with the decision for Lola to be a stay-at-home mom. I selfishly wanted to keep up with the Joneses. Material lust clouded my judgment.

But we stood by our decision. I committed to the worth of my family over the amount of my paycheck. We didn't experience the heartache parents have when dropping their kids off at daycare. Lola saw Elijah stand up the first time. She watched him take his first steps. She heard him speak his first word (dada). Lola cared for Elijah when he was sick. She created many wonderful memories with him. Trips to the park, the zoo, and play dates are forever etched in photos.

I created new memories at church. I experienced things with Elijah my dad didn't experience with me. I worshiped God with Elijah on my chest. When I preached, Lola coddled him. Others at the church loved on him too. Jesus showed me a new legacy our family would create.

I grew deeper in a relationship with Jesus. In the summer of 2010 Lola and I dedicated Elijah. Several family and friends came to support us. Some loved Jesus, some didn't know Him. We had our highest one-day attendance. When I preached the sermon, glimpses of my potential flashed before me. I began to see beyond myself. God could use me, if I was willing and available.

I yearned for more. I knew where Jesus wanted to take me. But Connection Point Church plateaued. It reached the ceiling of growth, a fact I did not want to face. The loyalty in my heart wanted to stay. But my head said to go. The thought of telling Aaron nauseated me.

I "grew up" in Connection Point Church. I stepped out of fear and preached. I studied the Word. I discovered the freedom in worship. I learned about the power and intimacy in prayer. I led people to the Lord. I dedicated my son there. My wife and I were baptized by Pastor Aaron.

God used Pastor Aaron to breathe life into me. He plucked me out of my spiritual bog. He raised me up in the church. He mentored me. He taught me many aspects of a personal walk with Jesus. He left an indelible impact on my life.

How could I abandon Pastor Aaron? I was sold out for his vision. I said yes to him the day he announced his church. In June 2011 our wonderful journey with Connection Point Church ended.

We left without a plan. We didn't have another church home. I thought, *Now what?* We attended Sunday service at several different churches. None seemed like a place we could plant roots.

For almost two months my hope deflated. I backslid into hopelessness. I descended deeper into the recesses of my mind. It seemed my Connection Point years were pointless. I challenged God. *Did you spend these last five years pulling me out of a pit just to let me fall back in? What happened to all the prophetic words you spoke over me? Where are your promises now God?*

My attitude and actions reflected my thoughts. My wife recognized my state of mind. She said, "I don't like where you are right now. It's like you went back to that place again." The gloom I wrapped around me infected my family.

July arrived. I desperately awaited my annual camping trip. My friends and I chose a new campground—Salmon La Sac, Washington. I relied on my camping trip to alleviate the constriction of my mind. I counted on it to provide relief and reprieve. I depended on it to help me escape.

The opposite happened. I remained a hostage. My spiritual prison expanded. I listened to depressing songs. I fixated on my inadequacies and mistakes. The alcohol and music created a toxic concoction. I attained no freedom on the trip.

I left the campground on a Sunday. The yearly countdown to the next camping trip began. Once in cell phone coverage my phone lit up with voicemails. I knew something bad had happened. As I listened to the messages, worry consumed me.

My brother needed help. The crisis hurt my heart. My sister and I took a red-eye down to South Carolina Monday night. We arrived to find him distraught and broken. I recognized his struggle and pain. We helped my brother make the decision to move back to Washington State.

I met a local pastor, Mark Lampley. He brought guys from his church and they cleaned my brother's house after he left. They hauled away leftover furniture and belongings. Mark encouraged me. He confirmed words Jesus spoke over me. I admired his self-less act of service to complete strangers. We packed my brother's belongings in a U-Haul within a few days.

When I first arrived I couldn't figure out why God wanted me there. Confused I wondered, *How can I help my brother? I am in the same state of mind he is. How useful can I be?*

Jesus gently answered me. *Do you see how my children are suffering? Are you willing to love, support and fight for them? I've called you to be a lighthouse in a world of darkness.*

His loving response turned my attention away from my own trouble. He helped me get my eyes off myself. He turned my heart towards others. Jesus brought back to my remembrance the promises He made.

I left South Carolina a changed man. His assignment for my life became clearer: be a voice of hope in His name.

Jesus brought me back to the story of Joseph. He showed me the treasure in Genesis 39 and Genesis 40. Joseph faced extreme injustice and huge obstacles in his life. But despite them, he turned his attention to other people's struggles. He focused on their needs. He helped them in their times of trouble.

Jesus presented me with opportunities to do the same. In October 2012 I traveled to San Diego. I attended a technology convention for work. I ran into a former co-worker. We hadn't seen each other for a while. We grabbed a bite to eat. He knew the Word well. He carried a strong apologetic disposition.

We talked and he shared his tough times with me. He stated he felt far away from God. I just listened to him. I simply identified with him. In the midst of our conversation God nudged me. *Remind him of who he is to me.* I obeyed. My friend's downcast demeanor melted away.

A quick meal turned into a spiritual resuscitation. He walked away recharged, boosted, and uplifted. He sent me a text later thanking me. I thanked Jesus. *I am slowly understanding Lord.*

I returned home. Seven weeks passed since I departed Connection Point Church. I became impatient and had reached a point of just picking a church. But, thank God, Lola didn't listen to me. She didn't want to rush the process. She remained committed to finding a church we could plant roots in.

One Saturday night in August 2011 my wife and I discussed our next church visit. I argued about where to go on Sunday. A friend from Connection Point found Canyon Creek Church. She recommended it. I put my foot down. "We are going to Canyon Creek Church tomorrow and that's final."

Lola and I arrived Sunday nervous and anxious. Thoughts conflicted my decision. *This better be the one, I am getting impatient. God, is this where you want us?* We walked in. Like deer in headlights we looked around. A guy smiled and greeted us. He wore a striped referee shirt. "Nice to meet you, are you new to our church?"

"Yes, this is our first time," we answered.

He genuinely seemed interested in our conversation. He then explained the referee jerseys were worn by all the ushers. He walked us to a seat. After service he invited us to join his growth group (small group).

We quickly discovered a church full of people like him—people who genuinely cared and welcomed us. The worship and teaching amazed us. I knew in my heart we were home. But I didn't say yes after one Sunday. We attended the next four services to be certain. After one month, Canyon Creek became the home our hearts longed for.

We committed to the mission God laid on our pastor's heart. We thrived in the atmosphere and we established relationships through our growth group. We connected with the entire staff. We fit in with our new family.

God cultivated the ground in my heart. He prepared me for the things He promised. I served in different areas. I lead growth groups. One day Pastor Christian approached me. "The Holy Spirit laid on my heart for you to be a part of the growth group leadership team. You would be a part of a team responsible for the overall growth group ministry."

I told him I would think and pray about it. But, inside, doubt and fear answered. *There's no way I can do that. I am not qualified. I haven't even been at the church one year.* But the Holy Spirit encouraged me. After a few weeks I accepted.

But I announced my inadequacy and lack of qualifications in the first meeting. "I am surprised Christian asked me to join this team. I haven't even been at the church a year. I feel like I don't have the right to be here."

But I grew tremendously over the two years I served. God blessed me with wisdom. Christian taught me leadership skills. I made some great relationships. I helped people connect together, grow in their faith, and serve the community. I began to remove roadblocks I built against God.

My journey towards freedom drew closer.

CHAPTER NINETEEN

A Giant Step for Me

BY NOVEMBER 2012, Lola and I celebrated her pregnancy of our second child. Excitement, fear, and worry filled our thoughts again. Lola battled fears with her previous trauma. Inadequacies as a father filled my mind. But we thanked Jesus. Elijah would be a big brother.

We spread the good news to friends and family. But a short time later Lola miscarried. We were devastated, especially Lola. She battled guilt and depression. Outbursts of anger and resentment consumed Lola. She carried the burden of the miscarriage for a long time.

I blamed myself. Punishment for my sinful past and my shortcomings as a father to Elijah. I failed my wife. I disappointed her. I didn't deserve to be a dad again.

But in the midst of questioning God, He helped me trust Him. I found comfort in His Word. He directed me to a teaching series by David Jeremiah called *Revealing the Mysteries of Heaven*. I discovered the beauty of 2 Samuel 12:22-23. I found peace in verse 23; "I will go to him." Jesus also pointed me to other people who shared similar stories—people like Pastor Robert Morris whose family went through several miscarriages.

My increased intimacy with Jesus made it harder to reject Him; harder to resist the freedom I desperately wanted; harder to tolerate my inner turmoil. My strength I once relied on failed me. Jesus pursued me. He broke down the barriers between us.

I tried everything to be free by my own power. But no evidence existed. College didn't rescue me. Friendships didn't sustain me. A strong physical body didn't protect me. Tattoos, earrings, jewelry and clothing didn't give me identity. Career, awards, sports and titles didn't make me whole. A wife and a son didn't complete me.

Incredible growth happened in 2013. God pushed me out of my comfort zone. He positioned me to mature. In late January I wrote the first words of my book. I served in different areas of the church. I participated in men's ministry events. Pastor Brandon, the lead pastor for Canyon Creek, approached me. He invited me to be a part of a group of guys he would mentor.

Again, doubt and question marks dominated my response. *The lead pastor of this church wants to spend one-on-one time with me? He thinks I should be a leader?* When the group of guys met the first day, I tried to measure up. I needed to prove myself. I figured I didn't have enough experience and credentials to qualify.

But Jesus never abandoned His promises to me. My lack of faith never altered His faithfulness. My passion for the Word increased. Sermons like "You ARE Salt and Light" from Pastor Christian burned inside me.

I listened to a sermon by Pastor Steven Furtick on identity. He focused on the interaction between Peter and Jesus in Matthew 16:13-20. Jesus had to first establish in Peter's mind who Jesus was before Peter could understand who Peter was:

Question: "Who do you say I am?"

Answer: "You are the Messiah, the Son of the living God."

Declaration: "And I tell you that you are Peter."

The sermon finished. My identity crisis weakened.

The momentum continued. Lola and I visited the Tri-Cities one weekend in February. Friends arranged for us to meet Prophet Clyde Lewis of Lewis Ministries International. I didn't know what to expect.

We sat and faced each other. He spoke of deep-rooted wounds in my life. He spoke about my future. His words confirmed the words of Pastor Aaron from years ago. Many profound statements and declarations were made.

Prophet Clyde said, "Bill, there are people waiting for you to be obedient to the Lord so they can be saved. I heard the Lord say, *I will bless your socks off the moment you say yes to me.* I cowered when I heard Prophet Clyde say those things.

He continued. "I hear the Lord saying, 'You have been on my heart for a long time. I'm here to tell you, you need to walk in the anointing and ministry I have for you.' But I hear the Lord say, 'You got to break the spirit of fear, rejection, and abandonment.' I also keep hearing the Lord say, 'Shame, grief, and sorrow.' I hear him saying, 'Loss of father, loss of father, fatherless.'"

The Holy Spirit revealed the magnitude of abandonment. The depths of rejection surfaced. Lack of intimacy with my dad appeared. Resentment towards my adoption bubbled up. I left the Tri-Cities challenged and shaken. The experience reminded me of when Pastor Aaron told me to stop wandering the corridors of my mind.

Jesus brought me to the story of Jonah. I knew the truth. I couldn't deny it. But I ran from God. I tried to escape what He wanted me to do. I evaluated my decision to run. I pondered the work Jesus did through me before.

He used me to preach the Word at Connection Point Church. He taught me how to lead small groups. He blessed me with opportunities to minister to groups of people. He stood by my side when I performed the memorial services for three of my grandparents.

People commented after the memorial services. "Are you a pastor? You should teach God's Word. You have a gift."

A friend of the family pulled me aside. With tears in her eyes she said, "When the time comes that Jesus calls my husband home, I would like you to do his memorial service."

Every time God provided confirmation and validation, even when I received criticism. A Greek Orthodox woman accused me of blasphemy. She exclaimed, "How can Bill do a memorial service? Is he ordained? These are last rites. He's not a minister."

Still, I tried to convince Jesus I wasn't who He said I was. I strained to prove to Him I couldn't do what He said I could do. My wrestling match with God wore me out, but transformation in my life persisted.

Sermons and wisdom from pastors substantiated God's truth. Reinhard Bonnke's *Full Flame* Film Series lit me up. God sent him to Africa to preach the Gospel. Many times he preached to just five people. But God soon used him to preach the gospel to over 50-percent of the population of Gaborone.

Jesus's pursuit of my heart never ceased. In early spring Pastor Yvonne of Christ the King Ministries entered my life. My wife and I knew of her, but we didn't know her personally. After a typical Sunday service ended, she walked right up to me. She said, "I have to tell you something. While we were worshipping, the Holy Spirit showed me your face. He revealed to me these chains wrapped around your body. But not normal-sized chains, the huge kind of chains they use for the anchors on a cruise ship or aircraft carrier."

I stood wide eyed and shocked. Over the next couple months I learned more about her. I discovered her passion for deliverance. She dedicated her life to helping people live free from bondage and chains.

A few months after our encounter, Pastor Brandon taught a new sermon series. God gave him a vision to plant 100 churches before he dies. I sat down with him for lunch one Sunday after church. He shared his heart and vision for the church. He searched for people committed to advancing the Kingdom. He wanted the Gospel to spread rapidly. My imagination ignited. My heart raced.

He prepared to fly down to Arizona. Some cities there were experiencing explosive growth—an excellent opportunity to plant a church or churches. He didn't explicitly ask if I would be willing to move to Arizona. But he planted a seed. What would my response be to the vision he cast?

Initially, I was unresponsive. Long before I attended Canyon Church I vowed never to live in Arizona or Texas. I had expressed my stance to God many times. He knew my reason why. It turned out I didn't get to tell God what to do.

For the next week the Holy Spirit relentlessly bugged me about Arizona. He highly encouraged me to say yes. I argued with Him during my commute. "But Lord, you know I don't want to move to Arizona. We've already had this conversation. I've already told you no before."

The following weekend I joined my first men's retreat. We gathered in a campground near Mount St. Helens, Washington. Dave Cole, the assistant superintendent of Northwest Ministry Network of the AG, shared his testimony. He pastored a church for twenty years. Well established and on cruise control, he wasn't looking for a change. Then God pushed him out of his comfort zone. Someone suggested he put his name in to be elected for the assistant superintendent position. He refuted God. He battled internally. But after while he said yes. New growth exploded in his life afterwards.

Pastor Russ Jorgenson, a former pastor at Canyon Creek, shared his testimony also. God lead his family to Kelso, Washington, to pastor a church. They arrived to find an unorganized church. A church in disarray. He didn't enjoy the services. He told God, "No way this is where you want us." But a series of divine events changed their hearts. He and his wife Rhonda are now the head pastors at Kelso Christian Assembly.

Around 6:30 the next morning I walked to a dock on the lake. I stood at the end of the dock facing Mount St. Helens. The sun had already risen and mist hovered over the water. A gentle breeze blew on my face. In the quiet the Holy Spirit whispered, *They said yes to me. Will you say yes to me too, Bill?*

I had stressed for over a week prior to His words. *What about my job?* I excelled at my career, worked hard at T-Mobile, and had built a solid reputation. I had received several awards and recognitions. God promoted me several times.

What about finances? What will Lola do? What about Elijah and school? What about the strange wildlife there, nasty spiders and bugs? A deluge of what-ifs and what-abouts bombarded my mind.

I pulled my digital recorder out of my pocket. I listened to my recorded conversation with Prophet Clyde. I shouted across the lake, "If God says so, it will be so." After my declaration the Lord filled me with scripture. He reminded me of Abraham's heart in Genesis 12:1-4. He packed up everything he owned. He moved to a strange land. The Bible contains no reference of hesitation, questioning comment or argument. He went because God said so.

Jesus showed me how the disciples reacted in a similar fashion. He tapped them on the shoulder and said, "Follow me." They immediately followed Him. There weren't any debates about the future. There's no reference to what-ifs and what-abouts.

But I still hesitated. The new dreams and visions God imparted clashed with my doubt and fear. He again addressed my weakness. I reread 1 Kings 19. Elijah ran from fear of Jezebel. He hid inside caves. 1 Kings 19:9 says, "And the word of the Lord came to him: 'What are you doing here, Elijah?'"

I had read that story and verse before, but the Holy Spirit spoke directly to me. *Bill, what are you doing still hiding in the caves of your mind? Why are you hiding from the promises I have for you? What do you fear? Don't you know I am for you and nothing can stand against you? Get out of the cave, Bill.*

Many breakthroughs happened during the men's retreat. On Sunday afternoon my family picked me up. We drove to the Oregon Coast for our yearly family reunion. While there, Pastor Yvonne called me. She said, "I feel like the Holy Spirit wanted me to call you and talk to you." I told her about my meeting with Clyde in February. I shared the discussions I had with Pastor Brandon. I explained my experience at the men's retreat.

She made another profound statement. "The Lord is saying, 'You fear a part of me that you don't know. Let go of the Bill that you know and give way to the Bill that I know.'"

My jaw dropped. My heart pounded. Another intimate and powerful encounter with Jesus. I left the Oregon Coast astonished.

Breakthrough continued the following weekend at my annual camping trip. Massive thunder and lightning storms hovered over the campground each night. I had feared thunder and lightning my entire life. Every few seconds a burst of lightning flashed across the sky. Sheet and bolt lightning rocked the mountains.

It illuminated my tent and the entire campground as if it were daytime. The wind rushed across the tree tops. The rain battered the tent. The rain sounded like water balloons on the tent. The deep thunder rumbled across the sky. The ground trembled and my bones shook.

I nestled my tent between a clump of giant pine trees. A huge branch broke off the tree above me. It landed about two feet from the tent. Friday night contained all the right ingredients for a potluck of fear.

By 2:00 a.m. I still couldn't sleep. Fear gripped and paralyzed me. I panicked. Anxiety smothered my chest. I closed my eyes and took a deep breath. I said, "Wait a minute. Lord, your Word says you tell every lightning bolt where to go and for it to report back to you. Your Word says you command the wind and you control the rain. Why should I be afraid when you are in complete control?"

The moment I said those words the peace of God settled all over me. I released a sigh. I smiled. I crushed my fear and anxiety. I praised Him and thanked Him. "Thanks for allowing me to experience and witness your power in creation." When a burst of lightning flashed I laughed, "Wow, Lord, how big was that lightning bolt? Wow, Lord, that one seemed like it was really close, cool. How many decibels was that thunder, Lord?"

Then I prayed a prayer with authority. "Lord, you control everything that's happening right now. And in the name of Jesus give your angels charge over me. No lightning bolt, no tree branch, nothing will harm this camp in Jesus name."

I slept wonderfully the remainder of the night. When the storm came again Saturday night, I remained relaxed and calm. Sources say that more than 600 lightning strikes were recorded that weekend.

Through the lightning storm Jesus helped me face my fear of trusting Him, fear of fully surrendering to Him, and the fear of letting go of the Bill Ker I knew. Jesus comforted my heart with Isaiah 43:18-19 (NKJV): "Do not remember the former things, nor consider the things of old. Behold, I will do a new thing, now it shall spring forth; shall you not know it? I will even make a road in the wilderness and rivers in the desert."

Another giant step towards my freedom.

CHAPTER TWENTY

Escape From Alcatraz

I REACHED THE zenith of disgust of my shackles. I no longer wanted to resist Jesus. I no longer wanted to call God a liar.

I shared my decision with Lola. "I am ready to be free. I am going to set up a meeting with Pastor Yvonne." She cried tears of joy. A few days later I called Pastor Yvonne. We set a time to meet.

In the time period before our meeting, I confronted my spiritual Alcatraz. I called it out. I exposed it. Jesus revealed what I had built for thirty-eight years. My Alcatraz didn't resemble the twenty-two-acre island in the middle of the San Francisco Bay.

It represented a giant island, so big it couldn't be fully explored. The corridors and cells stretched beyond sight. The dense foundation drove deep down into the earth. The bars were unbendable and unbreakable pillars. Impenetrable walls surrounded the compound. Thick as mountains. High as sky scrapers.

My Alcatraz lay in an endless black ocean. Violent currents and massive waves raged around it. The prison had no proximity to life. No city to look at. No trees to see in the distance. No civilization to bring hope or distraction.

A persistent fog absorbed the light. There were no inmates. No guards. No visitors. No amenities existed. No comfort. No food. No accommodations. No books to read. No physical activity.

Satan held me hostage inside. He bound me in perpetual solitary confinement. I remained trapped in isolation. A musty and dank odor permeated the prison. Hopelessness reverberated through the walls. Worthlessness saturated the corridors. Each day the vacuum of emptiness sucked the life out of me.

I built a fortress from which I was never meant to escape, a fortress with no means of rescue.

The day before my deliverance doubt plagued me. Satan tried to ensnare me. He tried to convince me I would lose the Bill Ker I knew. But the Holy Spirit shut him up. I pulled into a parking lot to get lunch. I sat in my truck and listened to a sermon by Pastor Chuck Swindoll with the title of "Clearing Away the Trash We Regret."

The Holy Spirit sweetly reminded me of His desire for reconciliation and restoration. I listened to the words from Joel 2:18-25, specifically, verse twenty-five, "I will give you back what you lost to the swarming locusts, the hopping locusts, the stripping locusts, and the cutting locusts. It was I who sent this great destroying army against you."

Jesus disarmed Satan's lie. He refreshed my spirit, my soul, and my body. He gave me final confirmation for my deliverance. I committed to be all in.

I prepared myself to give up everything Jesus wanted. The library of all my records of wrongs. All the cells I built and displayed like trophies in the prison of my mind. He wanted my account I created at the Bank of Despair. The account I used to deposit my failures and mistakes.

On August 20, 2013 at Canyon Creek Church, Pastor Yvonne lead me through deliverance. Lola stayed by my side. Pastor Yvonne held a piece of paper and pen. She asked me what I wanted to be free from. I spoke out and confessed the long list. She wrote everything down. No shame touched me when I did.

As I confessed, the Holy Spirit brought up my adoption. I didn't expect it. I couldn't figure out why. I never associated my struggles with my adoption before. The depths of my pain surfaced.

I asked Him questions. "I always wondered why was I adopted. Was I trash to them? Was I expendable? Was I worthless to them?" Each question shocked me. I said, "Wait, did I just say those things out loud? Where did those questions come from?" I sobbed.

The Holy Spirit revealed my adoption to Pastor Yvonne. He showed her the root, blueprint, and constructor of my prison. I didn't understand its hold on me. I didn't know the severity of the bondage.

Abandonment and rejection were the lieutenants of my stronghold. The weeds of deception that had rooted in my life created the breeding ground for all the other lies and torment in my life.

Pastor Yvonne shared a dream she had the morning of my deliverance. It was a dream about a little boy with dark hair and brown eyes. She described how she wanted to pick him up and hug him. She could see he desperately wanted love. But, as she tried, the little boy resisted. He lashed out in anger at the attempt of love. He pushed her away. He didn't allow her to get close.

Then she turned to me. "Bill, that little boy is you. You have been hurt for so long. You are angry and resistant to love because you've always felt abandoned and rejected."

God immediately revealed times when abandonment and rejection manifested. He showed me outbursts of anger at my biological parents. I remembered incidents when I lashed out at others.

Pastor Yvonne then addressed a root of pride in my life—pride in the prison I created—my lifetime achievement award. I built it. Nobody would tear it down. I insisted I owned my spiritual Alcatraz. The request to give it up seemed offensive. But when Jesus said, "It is finished," He meant it.

I placed myself in a position of humility. I lay out on the floor prostrate before Jesus, my palms relaxed and wide open. The little boy inside me needed to be healed first, then my grown-up man. Pastor Yvonne prayed over me. I closed my eyes. I stood at the top of the basement stairs in my Kennewick house. I stretched out my arms and said, "I love you Jesus Christ, God, good angels and guardian angels." Jesus walked towards me out of the darkness of the basement. He smiled at me. I embraced Him and said, "You were there the whole time. You were there all along."

Then my vision shifted to His throne room. He sat on a huge throne. I stood at His feet as an adult. The little boy stood next to me. I looked at him. Compassion flooded my heart. I told the little boy, "It's okay, you *are* loved." The little boy and I merged. Jesus made me whole.

Pastor Yvonne continued. I confessed my sins. I repented of the things I did to hurt Jesus. I renounced the lies I believed my entire life. I gave up being my own judge and record keeper of wrongs. I asked Jesus to forgive me.

The huge, aircraft-carrier anchor chains broke off me at the feet of Jesus. My old self came off like old tattered clothing. A sword appeared in my hands. I thrust it through the chains and tattered clothing. Then my attention turned towards my spiritual Alcatraz.

I knelt at the feet of Jesus. I could only see up to His knees. His hands rested on the arms of the throne. I looked over at my spiritual Alcatraz. Next to Jesus it appeared like a tiny box. It cowered in His presence. Pastor Yvonne warred against it. She commanded it to be destroyed.

I worried the destruction of my prison would take years. I imagined using a sledge hammer to dismantle it brick by brick or a wrecking ball to tear it down. But the power of God welled up inside me. I shouted at my spiritual Alcatraz with a voice of triumph. It disappeared instantly.

The breath of the Lord literally blew it into smithereens. Not a piece remained. He annihilated my spiritual Alcatraz. I pictured a ghost town scene from an old western movie. The wind wisped a small dust cloud. A tumbleweed bounced through an empty street.

Transparent gold bricks lay beneath where the foundation used to be. Jesus then lifted me up. He faced me away from Him. He showed me a horde of demons in front of me. With a rush of His mighty power He swept them away.

Then Pastor Yvonne transitioned me into a posture of receiving. Receiving a new life filled with purpose. Filled with the pursuit of Jesus and His truth. A challenge to dedicate my life to building a house for the Lord. I was no longer building a prison for the enemy.

When we finished I stood. Three hours had passed but seemed like three minutes. I took a deep breath. The straightjacket of lies no longer constricted me. New life rushed through me like I had plugged into a light socket. Strength rushed through my physical body.

Pastor Yvonne handed me the piece of paper. She declared, "Now take it and cut it up. Throw it away because Jesus has delivered you."

I burned the list.

CHAPTER TWENTY-ONE

The Real Bill Ker Stands Up

JESUS LIFTED THE tremendous weight from my heart. I breathed in 2 Corinthians 3:17 and 2 Corinthians 5:17. For the first time in thirty-eight years my eyes were opened. A new life outside my prison welcomed me. A dark cloud no longer hovered over me. I understood God's desire for sin and bondage to be a foreign feeling, not freedom and liberty.

Jesus revealed my true identity. He removed the blinders over my eyes. He exposed the lies spoken over me. He showed me the Bill Ker that He created me to be. He didn't take away my unique attributes. I didn't transform into a lifeless corpse or robot.

In the weeks and months immediately following my deliverance, I adjusted to my new life, similar to men who are released from prison after decades. They experience difficulties acclimating to the real world. After I escaped my dungeon, I discovered how deplorable it was. I didn't realize the putrid stench numbed my senses.

I stepped into a life of newness and wholeness. All aspects of my life changed. I cleaned up my thought life. My actions changed. I spoke life more often. My five senses were heightened and more sensitive.

I prayed with intention. I worshiped with intimacy. My one-on-one time with Jesus increased. I studied the Word with more passion. I began to remove barriers against the Holy Spirit. I allowed Him to flow and operate more freely in my life.

Celebrate Recovery provided a safe place to share my story. To other men, I confessed my struggles. I walked through the process of recovery. I discovered the beauty in James 5:16. I am still involved in Celebrate Recovery.

In the newness of my freedom I listened to a sermon—"Lighting the Future"—by Dr. Adrian Rogers. Dr. Rogers shared a story about a man who resisted God's will his entire life. One day he finally submitted. He prayed a simple but powerful prayer. "Lord, anytime, anywhere, any cost."

Those four words resonated in me. I pondered them. I examined my heart. I asked myself what relationship I wanted with Jesus. I trusted the promises in Jeremiah 29:11.

Lola and I agreed to move to Arizona. I met with Pastor Brandon for lunch after church at the end of August. I told him our plans to move to Arizona. I gave him our commitment to help plant a church. In October we visited Arizona for a weekend. We met with a realtor and I applied for jobs.

Our decision sparked mixed emotions from family and friends. Some were excited for us. Others were angry. Most reacted with utter shock. Lola's mom responded with tears. The distance from Washington broke her heart.

Many people questioned our decision. "Why do you want to leave everything behind? Don't you know how hot it gets there in the summer?" The questions were valid. We would pull up our roots. We didn't have any family there. We didn't have any friends. We didn't know the culture. We would start new lives from scratch.

But we knew Jesus had a greater purpose for us there, one that could not be accomplished through us if we stayed. We anchored our hearts into the promise of Mark 10:28-30.

In the end, we didn't move. The church delayed the launch of an Arizona campus. But we weren't discouraged. We learned to trust Him more. He built our faith through the process. He wanted to see if I was willing. He wanted to know what I was willing to give up. He wanted to test if I would go anywhere for Him. I couldn't have done any of it without my freedom.

Over the course of three years my walk with Jesus intensified. Satan tried multiple attempts to reestablish blueprints for a new prison. He tried to get me to revert to my old ways. I backslid sometimes. But I proceeded forward in my freedom.

When I made mistakes I didn't run and hide in my prison. I declared, "I am not going back. Jesus said, 'It is finished.'" I took accountability for my mistakes. I apologized when I could. I moved on.

I dealt with my triggers with a fresh perspective. My wife and I watched the movie *Lone Survivor*. The enemy attacked my mind the entire time. He stirred up old thoughts of guilt and condemnation. "You should have joined the military." He tried to seduce me. He tried to lure me to build a new prison.

His attack stunned me. For a moment I considered his words. The movie ended and we walked out of the theater. While we discussed some of the scenes, Lola could see the mental battle on my face. She said, "Now listen, don't go back to that place. Don't let those thoughts back in." We stopped the onslaught with 2 Corinthians 10:5.

For thirty-eight years my birthday reminded me of the mistake I thought God made, a regurgitation of my weaknesses. I used to compare my birthday to what Job said in Job 3:1-10. I regretted all my previous birthdays. I despised them. But I celebrated my thirty-ninth birthday. I celebrated the new hope it represented. I approach each birthday with a new attitude.

Compliments were easier to receive. I accepted them without condemnation. They weren't laced with guilt. Shame didn't precede accolades. I thanked God on behalf of my awards and recognition.

Jesus restored the years of friendship robbery. He redeemed the joy of relationships. I turned my "friendship switch" on. I understood the meaning of fellowship. Scriptures like Ecclesiastes 4:9-12 watered the parched desert of my past.

I created numerous new relationships and strengthened existing ones. I interacted better with people in general and no longer withdrew from social interaction. I craved a sense of community, and starved myself of isolation. I told Lola, "Before, I could count my friends at church on one hand. Now, every time we go to church there isn't enough time for me to talk with everyone I love."

I didn't lift weights to carry burdens anymore. I didn't adorn myself with jewelry, clothing, or other things to seek value. I didn't hide behind my tattoos. I enjoyed music without ulterior motives. The agenda to crush myself through sad songs has deteriorated. The grip of "performance equals value" fades each day. The mirror isn't a disgusting thing anymore. The urge to impress people lessens as time passes.

My new freedom changed my prayer life. I prayed with more authority, confidence, and faith. I prayed for a friend's old ACL injury from sports. After church he approached me. "Hey Bill, my knee feels great. I am walking up and down these stairs without any pain. It's like it healed. It's weird, I don't remember the last time my knee felt good."

I responded with elation and surprise. "Wow, God really *can* use me." I focused on scriptures such as 2 Chronicles 16:9 (NLT): "The eyes of the Lord search the whole earth in order to strengthen those whose hearts are fully committed to Him."

I worshipped with a new hunger. I praised Him and exalted Him from a place of thanksgiving, not a place of disgrace. Tears I shed were from the joy of the Lord, not from worthlessness. I eagerly awaited our Wednesday night worship service called OneVoice. Pastor Di challenges us to stretch ourselves, get out of our comfort zones and truly worship God.

The Holy Spirit opened my eyes to the impact my deliverance will have on others. And I would do it from a place of peace. I no longer shouted over the thunderstorms of sorrow. I understood the message in 2 Corinthians 2:1-2.

Jesus put me to work. I spoke to a good friend of mine from college on the phone. He had suffered so much tragedy and disappointment over the course of a few years that he had reached his breaking point. He told me, "I don't know what to do anymore Bill." I encouraged him the best I could. The phone call ended.

The next day I prayed for him on my commute. The Lord said to me, *I will bless Him, but he needs to lay down his pride first. Tell him he needs to lay down his pride.* I wondered, *How will he react to this? I will feel a bit silly telling him.*

But, I did as the Lord said. I called him a few days later. We chatted for a bit. I cut to the chase. "Well, let me tell you the real reason why I called. I have been thinking about you. My heart was breaking for you so I prayed–"

"Oh wow," he interrupted, "I was going to ask you to pray for me the last time we chatted. But I felt dumb asking."

I whispered to myself, "Sorry for doubting you Lord." I then told him what Jesus said to me. My friend proceeded to reveal feelings of anger and bitterness. He harbored unforgiveness and resentment. He couldn't sleep. He lost his appetite. I told him, "Write down on a piece of paper all the things you shared with me. All the things that are consuming your mind and life. Then find a quiet place so it's just you and God. No distractions. Get on your knees and lay the paper down as if you were laying it down at His feet. But before you ask anything, lay down your pride. Then lay down all the other things. He wants you to give it all to Him because it was already crucified on the cross and buried."

He e-mailed me the next day. The e-mail read: "I did what you said . . . I wrote it down and thought about things and talked to Him. I asked for His help, I gave away all this negativity, and I asked to know what path I need to take. I want the life I had before and the man I was. I want its meaning and what it provided for me and for others, but if not, I want to know what to do, what path to take."

I began to understand my deeper purpose. I remembered the words of Prophet Clyde Lewis "There are people waiting for you to be obedient so they can be saved."

I discovered the "Bill Ker" Jesus created me to be.

I discovered my true identity.

CHAPTER TWENTY-TWO

I Am Never Going Back

THE GOD WHO delivered me from the corridors of my mind is real. His love is greater than anything humans can understand. Far greater than any mathematical equation could calculate. More magnificent than any artist's painting. More beautiful than the most beautiful song.

The Bible says Jesus perceives every thought from afar. He knows every word before it's on your tongue. He records your laments. He lists your tears on His scroll. He has numbered each hair on the top of your head.

Jesus wants you to know Him. He wants to have an intimate and personal relationship with you. Psalm 139:1-10 says He already knows everything about you. He is standing at the door of your heart, knocking, knocking. He wants you to let Him in. He is the only true life and freedom.

No matter what your situation, circumstance, or things you have done in life, you can't buy His love. You can't work enough to earn His love. You can't give enough to earn His love. You can't be nice enough to earn His love. You can't be good enough to earn His love. Jesus has given you the free gift of grace.

You may not fully understand all you read in this book. You may still have many questions. That's okay. But, if you don't know Jesus, you will never know who you are. You will never know your true identity. You will spend a lifetime searching for your value. The black hole in your heart will consume everything and never be satisfied.

Only Jesus gives you an identity. No one and nothing can take it away from you. If you have never accepted Jesus Christ into your life as your Lord and Savior you can do that now.

Wherever you are now, you can find Him. In the airport. On your front porch. In a hotel room. In a bar. He's there. There's no defined script to get Jesus. No religious ritual. No religious proceeding. The Bible says when you believe in your heart and confess with your mouth that Jesus is Lord, you will be saved.

Read these words aloud. Sincerely mean them in your heart. Jesus will come and live inside you.

Lord Jesus Christ, I come before You today tired of being held prisoner in my life and in my mind. I am broken. I've made mistakes and I desperately need You. I ask You to forgive me of all of my sins. Wash me clean and make me new. I ask You to come into my heart and into my life. From this day forward I make You my Lord and Savior. Thank You for saving me. Thank You for rescuing me. Thank You for loving me. Thank You for giving me an identity. Because of Your love and forgiveness I am now free. In Jesus' name. Amen.

If you are a Christian, don't wait to be free. The time is now. Write down the list of things in your life that have kept you prisoner. Go to a quiet, private place where you are alone with God. Get in a position of humility, on your knees, or on your face, whatever posture puts you in a position to lay everything down before Him. Present that list to Jesus. Confess your sins. Repent for the things that separated you from Him.

Tell Him from your heart you only want the identity He gave you. Tell Jesus you receive affirmation, validation, and value from

Him alone. Ask Jesus for the fullness of God to fill your life. Ask for the freedom He gave you. Let His Holy Spirit wash over you. Let Him make you white as snow.

Then take that list and burn it. Pursue Jesus. Seek His face. Stay connected to your brothers and sisters in the body. Find a Celebrate Recovery near you. Find someone who has experience in deliverance ministry. Investigate ministries of other Christians who have experienced the freedom of Christ, free men like Todd White.

Friends, Jesus delivered me. I am never going back into my spiritual Alcatraz. It's not there anymore. It will never be built again. I no longer call God a liar.

Jesus still has much refining to do in my life. I battle daily to deny my flesh. I continue to submit the lust of my eyes and selfish desires to Jesus. He continues to show me wounds that haven't fully healed. Deeper level healing awaits me because He wants all of me.

But I fight not to allow the voice of my carnal mind to shout over the triumphant voice of truth. I refuse to allow the enemy to stomp life out of me. Now I make it my mission to stomp hell. I now have a mission to reclaim what the enemy stole from me and my brothers and sisters in Christ.

I am more open and available to be used by Jesus. I am embracing who God called me to be in Isaiah 6:8 and Isaiah 52:7.

May you know the friend we have in Jesus. May you walk with Him all the days of your life. You were not created to be a prisoner, but to walk victoriously in the freedom of Christ.

Now, go forth and Stop Wandering the Corridors of *Your* Mind.

Contact Information

To order additional copies of this book, please visit
www.redemption-press.com.
Also available on Amazon.com and BarnesandNoble.com
Or by calling toll free 1-844-2REDEEM.

CPSIA information can be obtained
at www.ICGtesting.com
Printed in the USA
FSOW02n0340280817
37967FS